I BOUGHT A BUS

A MEMOIR

BY BELINDA ADAMS

A story of love, resilience, recovery and adventure

First published in Australia in 2024

Copyright © Belinda Adams 2024 – For more information please visit www.citrinesunentertainment.com

All rights reserved. No part of this book may be reproduced or transmitted in any form or by any means, electronic or mechanical, including photocopying, recording or by any information storage and retrieval system without prior permission in writing from the publisher.

The author and publisher have made all reasonable efforts to contact copyright-holders for permission and apologise for any omissions or errors in the form of credits given.

Acknowledgement and Clarification

This memoir is a work of non-fiction. The events, experiences, and characters depicted are based on my personal recollections and interpretations. Some names and identifying details have been changed to protect the privacy of individuals. Any resemblance to actual persons, living or dead, or actual events is purely coincidental if not explicitly stated otherwise.

The views expressed in this manuscript are my personal narrative and perspective and should not be considered an objective account of events. They reflect my personal experiences and interpretations at the time of writing. They do not necessarily represent the views or opinions of any other individuals or organisations.

The purpose of this memoir is to share my personal journey and insights with readers. It is not intended to serve as professional advice or instruction. Readers seeking guidance on specific issues should consult a qualified professional.

Content Warning

This memoir addresses complex, sometimes sensitive topics and trauma which some readers may find distressing.

Final Note

I hope that by sharing my story, I can contribute to a broader understanding of the human experience. I am grateful to all those who have been a part of my journey and to the readers who take the time to engage with my narrative.

Thank you for your understanding and respect for the nuances of personal storytelling.

Distributed by Bellflower Books

ISBN 978 1 7636584 0 0

This project is supported by the Regional Arts Development Fund (RADF). RADF is a partnership between the Queensland Government and Logan City Council to support arts and culture in regional Queensland.

Cover Photograph © Ben Craig - Synapse 2017

For **Dylan, Mikaela & Hudson**
The rhythm of your hearts inspired the lyrics of my life...

Dedicated to the loving memory of Chell and Ronny Campbell
No Fear.... No Regrets.... No surrender!

Contents

Foreword ———————————————————————— 1

CHAPTER ONE ——————————————————————— 3
What is Fear?

CHAPTER TWO ——————————————————————— 13
Tick Tock

CHAPTER THREE —————————————————————— 27
Is it Better to Give False Hope or False Despair?

CHAPTER FOUR ——————————————————————— 43
Do You Know Who I Am?

CHAPTER FIVE ———————————————————————— 59
Please Help

CHAPTER SIX ————————————————————————— 73
Mr Downey If You Please

CHAPTER SEVEN ———————————————————————— 89
Life as Lyrics

CHAPTER EIGHT ———————————————————————— 105
I Bought a Bus

CHAPTER NINE — 117
Menindee Sky

CHAPTER TEN — 133
End of an Era

CHAPTER ELEVEN — 147
Chasing Jon

CHAPTER TWELVE — 165
Robbed and Rolled

CHAPTER THIRTEEN — 173
I Grieved

CHAPTER FOURTEEN — 183
You Couldn't Make This Shit up

CHAPTER FIFTEEN — 195
School's Out

CHAPTER SIXTEEN — 205
Seismic Life

CHAPTER SEVENTEEN — 223
Belinda's Big Bus Tour

CHAPTER EIGHTEEN — 245
Dancing with the Darkness

CHAPTER NINETEEN ———————————————— 259
Buckleys

CHAPTER TWENTY ————————————————— 275
Banging The Drum

CHAPTER TWENTY-ONE ———————————————— 297
Back to the Bush

CHAPTER TWENTY-TWO ———————————————— 309
Ballet for Brain Injury

Acknowledgements ————————————————— 325

Endorsements —————————————————————— 328

Foreword

'This is going to be a long journey,' the nurse in the ICU told Belinda Adams as she sat by her son's bedside. Those words, meant as a warning, became a profound truth that resonated deeply with her. In her memoir, Belinda captures the unimaginable reality of living with brain injury, a journey that is far from over even as she shares her story with us in this book. Brain injury consumes everything, demanding strength, resilience, and a relentless spirit to navigate the unpredictable highs and lows. For those who have lived with it, Belinda's vivid recounting brings the memories rushing back; for those who haven't, it offers a rare glimpse into the raw and turbulent emotions that define this journey. Belinda writes with a clarity and honesty that makes the reader feel every moment, every uncertainty, and every hope.

As Belinda narrates her journey with Dylan, she lays bare the cracks in our health, rehabilitation, and disability systems—systems riddled with bureaucratic obstacles that often lack compassion and understanding. She doesn't shy away from revealing her own struggles, including moments of anger and despair that reflect the immense pressure she faced. Yet, through her candour, we gain insight into the profound love and fear that fuel such emotions. She also honours the compassionate individuals who, in the midst of this chaos, offer support so valuable that it lingers in our memory long after the crisis has passed.

Belinda's story is not just one of resilience; it is a story of triumph. Her ability to turn every challenge into an opportunity for positive change is truly inspiring. From her Big Bus awareness campaign, creative initiatives like the Ballet for Brain Injury and the Biggest Beanie to her endless advocacy efforts with politicians, Belinda demonstrates that even in the darkest times, we can find a way to make a meaningful impact. Her journey, and brain injury itself, teach us all that life's uncertainties demand we live fully and with purpose. Belinda, your strength and dedication inspire us all to live more boldly and with greater passion. Thank you for writing this book.

Professor Elizabeth Kendall AM,
Griffith University, August 2024

CHAPTER ONE

What is Fear?

March 14, 2012, a date I will never forget. I was sitting in the crowded departure lounge at Adelaide Airport, awaiting my flight to Broken Hill, my hometown in Far Western New South Wales.

I probably cut a lonely figure against the great wall of glass, mesmerised by the ominous sky, the dark clouds moving towards me. My initial feelings of excitement about my holiday to visit family and friends had disappeared. I was overcome with an overwhelming feeling of impending doom.

I heard the announcement over the PA inviting us to board our flight, so I sent Dylan (nineteen), the eldest of my three children, a quick message saying I love you, turned my phone to flight mode, and boarded the little Rex Airlines SAAB 340B.

The 340B took off as the sky delivered on its promise, opening up a torrential downpour on the tiny aircraft. As the plane gained altitude, the captain came over the intercom informing us we needed to fly slightly off course to avoid lightning strikes, so our landing time would be later than scheduled. I sat at my window seat watching the lightning move further into the distance. The roar of thunder matched the pounding of my heart and I just couldn't shake the feeling that something was terribly wrong. I found myself trembling as a cold chill made me wonder if we were going to make our destination at all.

I closed my eyes, picturing the small plane surrounded by a ball of protective white light. Eventually, the storm eased and the clouds cleared to reveal the familiar site of red desert plains and we descended smoothly into Broken Hill.

Outside the arrivals lounge I looked for the familiar faces of my cousin Rebekah, the same age as me and more like a sister, and one of my oldest and dearest friends Rachel. Rach rushed forward to hug me, balancing her daughter Isabelle, almost two, on her hip. It didn't feel like a normal welcome hug. Something was terribly wrong. Rach released me from her embrace and a heavily pregnant Rebekah took hold of my shoulders, looked me straight in the eyes and said, 'I have some bad news. Dylan has been in a bad car accident.'

My throat tightened. I struggled to breathe and a voice I barely recognised as my own whispered, 'How bad is it?'

'He has multiple injuries, but most concerning is the head injury. He's in the ICU in an induced coma.'

I felt like the wind had been knocked out of me. I needed to get back home to Brisbane to my boy but there were no flights out until the following day, and there are no direct flights from Broken Hill to Brisbane, so getting home would require a connecting flight to either Adelaide again or Sydney. Bek and Rach had already run through every scenario to get me home fast, but it wouldn't be until the following morning via Sydney.

'You need to know, there's a possibility that he may not survive the night,' Bek said, using her years of experience as a nurse to deliver this news calmly. It must have been one of the hardest conversations of her life.

Moments passed. I stood rooted to the concrete path outside the airport arrivals entrance, blinking rapidly, trying to process what I had heard. The luggage cart whizzed by and I barely noticed. I reached into my pocket, pulled out my phone, and switched it on. The consistent buzzing of countless notifications coming through informed me of missed calls and texts received while I'd been flying.

The accident had occurred five minutes after take-off in Adelaide. My sense of foreboding had been correct, but it wasn't my life in danger, it had been Dylan's. With trembling hands, I called my mum as I somehow made it through the airport to Rachel's car. Mum told me that Dylan had just been at the local shopping centre where he met up with friends and they headed off for an afternoon drive to Mount Gravatt Lookout.

It was raining. As they descended the mountain Dylan braked and the wheels locked up. The car aquaplaned straight off the side of the mountain, hitting a tree head on.

Thankfully the only passenger walked out of the car unharmed, but Dylan had to be cut from the wreckage by emergency services before being rushed to the hospital in an ambulance.

In Broken Hill we made our way through the wide streets lined with heritage- listed buildings and miners' cottages. I loved this town but the familiar feelings of the isolation of this remote outback location hit me tenfold. I reconciled the fact that I was stranded here overnight with no way home to my boy.

Mikaela, my middle child, and Hudson the youngest were at home with mum, highly distressed. Mikaela begged me to let her go to the hospital: 'Everyone is trying to protect me,' she said, 'but I want to be there for Dylan. What if I don't get to see him again?' She cried into the phone, and I cried with her as she named my own greatest fear. I knew in my gut that if I couldn't be there, Miki was the next best thing. She was only seventeen at the time, but she was incredibly mature and strong, and extremely close to both her brothers.

'I think you need to be there too. You need to tell him I'm on my way and to hang on. You need to reassure him that he is going to be okay,' I told her.

As I ended the call, I realised we had arrived at Rachel's house. My phone continued to ring as news of Dylan's accident spread, but I was unable to respond to the overwhelming volume of messages. Bek had gone ahead to take care of my travel arrangements. In fact, she and Rachel had made an impromptu care plan for me before I landed: I would spend a few hours with Rach, her hubby Damo and Isabelle at their home, then they would drop me at Rebekah's later in the evening.

I had known Damo from the age of four when our parents lived across the road from one another. He and Rach were one of the few enduring love stories from high school, and the bonds of our friendship had only strengthened over the years. The reason I'd come home was to attend St Pats Raceday, one of Broken Hill's biggest social events with Rach and Tambi, another one of our old school gang. St Pats is a unique racing experience in outback NSW, drawing huge crowds of locals and visitors.

Those plans were now a distant memory. Instead, my friends, affectionately known as Aunty Rach and Uncle Damo to my kids, now tried to comfort and care for me. Damo served up a plate of fresh fish and steamed vegies but I couldn't digest more than a few bites. Rachel wrapped me up in one of her favourite blankets, which she then insisted I take with me to symbolise an ongoing embrace from them all.

At Bek's house, she had made up one of the boy's beds for me to sleep in, though needless to say neither of us got much sleep that night. My thoughts were with my son 1600 km away. There was a possibility he may not be alive when I got home, that I would never get to say goodbye.

I have never felt so helpless in my life.

It was still dark the following morning when we left for the airport. We were halfway there when Bek's car broke down. Like what the actual fuck! It was a race against time as we waited for Tambi to pick us up off the side of the road.

Tambi's old dual cab ute finally pulled up in front of us, and her gentle eyes mirrored my sadness. She planted her foot on the accelerator as soon as we climbed in, and the sense of urgency for me to make that flight gripped us all.

The ute came to a screeching halt in front of the airport. Bek and Tambi huddled around me, escorting me through the chilly, pre-dawn wind. Rachel's blanket was in my hand as I checked in at the counter. It felt like such a long time ago but in reality it was a mere twelve hours since I had landed at this same airport.

Tambi, not normally a hugger, gave me a hug that I felt right down to my soul. Bek joined in, and then we all cried as they waved me goodbye.

Rebekah had made the airport staff aware of my situation, and they ushered me gently onto the aircraft first, seating me right at the back so I could have what little privacy was possible on the cramped flight. As we taxied down the runway, the tears I had been holding for the past twelve hours poured out. I fumbled with the overhead vent, seeking some relief from the claustrophobia as if the small funnel of air was a reminder to breathe. I can't imagine how horrible this flight must have been for my fellow passengers, my gut-wrenching sobs invading the tiny space for the entire two-and-a-half-hour flight.

I kept seeing Dylan smiling as he dropped me off at Brisbane airport twenty-four hours earlier, kissing my cheek as I hopped out of his car saying, 'Love you mum, have a fun trip.' How life can change in an instant! Fear gripped me as endless scenarios ran through my mind: *what if something happens now and no one can contact me? Will I arrive to the worst possible news?* I closed my eyes, repeating in my mind *Dylan, I love you, I'm on my way, you are going to be okay. Dylan, I love you, I'm on my way, you are going to be okay.*

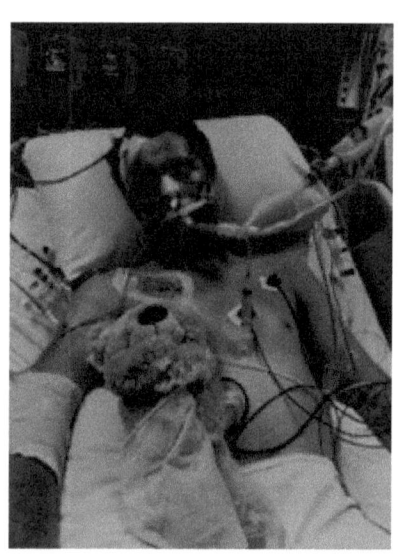

Dylan in the ICU

CHAPTER TWO

Tick Tock

As we landed in Sydney the other passengers were asked to stay in their seats so I could be escorted out first. I felt like a freak as I passed my fellow passengers, who had been forced to listen to me howling for the past two hours. They dropped their gaze as I was ushered past.

On the tarmac, the flight attendant led me to a car that took me straight to the check-in for my next flight to Brisbane. The short wait in the bustling and overcrowded Sydney departure lounge felt like an eternity until I was finally able to board my final flight, homeward to my boy.

My friend Chell – Michelle – was waiting for me in the arrivals area of Brisbane Domestic terminal. I descended the travellator two stairs at a time into her loving embrace. Ronny, Chell's husband, was out front in the pick-up zone ready to race me to the hospital. Ronny and Chell lived across the road from us, two of their four children were the same age as two of my own, so we'd become fast friends when the kids began preschool together many years earlier.

I dove into the rear passenger seat with my baggage still in hand as Chell explained that Dylan's condition hadn't changed. As we drove to the hospital she tried to prepare me for what I was about to experience but there are no words that can prepare you for seeing your child in a coma. The ICU waiting room was very full, not only with Dylan's family and friends but with all the other unlucky families on the same horrific journey. Mikaela rushed forward, throwing her arms around me. 'I kept telling him you were on your way, just like you asked me to,' she said.

'I'm so relieved you were here with him toots. How lucky he is to have you,' I said. She knew I was desperate to see Dylan, so she let me go.

I was shown the entry procedure: how to wash my hands and arms before entering the ICU. I was informed of the strict two-visitor rule: short, specified times only in intensive care.

I held my breath as I reached the end of the hallway. The sterile smell and endless beeping sounds from the machines that were keeping people alive hit my already frayed nerves as I rounded the corner.

A chill ran through my whole body as I caught sight of Dylan for the first time. His lifeless body was hooked up to all the life support machines that seemed to be breathing life into him. Tears slid down my face as I gently picked up his hand, kissed his cheek, whispered in his ear: 'I'm here mate, and I am not leaving here until you do.'

I nodded awkwardly at my ex-husband Paul who was sitting on the other side of Dylan's bed. It occurred to me that this was the first time I had seen him in months. The divorce was still fresh. It had only been two years since he came home from work one day and casually announced he was moving out, like he was asking me to pass him the salt. He had a new girlfriend, the second since our separation; we were all still finding our way in a changing landscape.

I felt a mixture of emotions, not least being the discomfort that he, who was now like a stranger to me, was there to witness the most vulnerable moment of anguish I had experienced as a mother. I pushed these feelings away. They were insignificant at a time like this. I turned my attention to Dylan and took in every inch of his bruised and battered body. His head was swollen and his hair had been shaved on one side where artificial instruments had been inserted into his brain. One of his arms was bandaged up and his naked body was covered by a sheet to protect his privacy.

I introduced myself to the nurse sitting at a desk beside Dylan's bed who was entering information into a computer.

'What are all these machines and cords for?'

He looked up from the monitor and explained that the respirator was helping Dylan to breathe, there was a shunt in his head to monitor the pressure and swelling in his brain, and they'd inserted a feeding tube down his nasal passage into his stomach, along with a central line into his chest.

A team of doctors entered the ICU and surrounded Dylan's bed. An older, clean-cut doctor who seemed to be leading the group picked up the patient clipboard as I asked for more information on Dylan's condition. He told me that Dylan's condition was very serious; he had several broken ribs, a fracture in his spine and a collapsed lung. But the most serious concern was the swelling in his brain.

His voice was monotone, as if he were reading out the contents of a shopping list.

'How severe is the head injury?' I asked.

'The thing with head injuries,' he said, 'is that we can't determine the extent of the damage this early on. When the brain has an impact like Dylan's has, we need to put the patient into an induced coma so the body can rest and have time to heal.' He said they were doing everything they could, but just couldn't predict the outcome this early on.

He hung up the clipboard and, with his team, moved on to the next patient. Despite what I had just been told, at that moment I had this overwhelming feeling that not only would Dylan survive, he would make a full recovery. There was no alternative.

I leant down and whispered in Dylan's ear: 'You are a fighter. I know you can hear me, and you need to know that you are going to be okay.'

Two wardsmen approached. The nurse instructed us to leave the room while they turned Dylan. We would receive a call in the waiting room to let us know when visitors could return. I gave Dylan a quick kiss on the cheek before Paul and I reluctantly left the ICU.

'I thought you would fall apart,' Paul said. To be honest, I thought I would too, but I suddenly felt a strength like I had never known before. I had no time to fall apart, I needed to be strong for Dylan. For us all.

I bypassed the waiting room, heading straight to the hallway near the lifts. The two rooms were separated only by walls of smoky glass, a big blue number 3 painted on the panels to indicate the floor level.

I needed to call my mum, Frannie. She was home with Hudson and answered my call immediately. I updated her on Dylan's condition, asking how Hudson was doing. She said she'd found him googling images of people in a coma, and he didn't want to come to the hospital because he feared seeing Dylan in that state.

I was unsure what to do. I certainly didn't want to push him into anything he wasn't comfortable with. He was only twelve, and I understood him being afraid, but I felt we needed to be together as a family and didn't like that he was separated from everyone else. But after a brief chat with him I realised he wasn't ready. I told him I loved him and promised to pass on his love to Dylan.

In the waiting room I made a beeline for the wall phone. It was the only connection from the waiting room to the ICU. I wasn't alone. It is the strangest thing to see all these people waiting for one phone to ring. Each time it rang, hopeful faces would stare intently at whoever had been closest and answered the call, waiting for them to announce which family the call was for. Everyone in the waiting room was in a highly emotional state, dealing with the trauma of someone they love being critically ill. It was a difficult place to be.

Later that night, as I sat beside Dylan, time seemed to stand still. Sitting beside your child not knowing if or when they will wake up and, if they do, wondering if they will know who you are, or even who they are, is the worst possible kind of waiting.

Growing up in the outback mining town of Broken Hill, I was a sporty and studious child. I was doing well at school until I hit the age of fourteen. Then I, along with many of my peers, bored with the lack of things to do in a small, isolated town (at least that is what we told ourselves), began wagging school and partying. We'd sneak out our bedroom windows at all hours, go to the pub with our fake IDs, and get drunk. Education was no longer a priority for me. One of my high school teachers tried to steer me towards my passion for writing, helping me put together a book of poetry to send to publishers in Sydney. He believed in me and dared me to believe in myself, but I didn't have the self-confidence or resilience required to overcome the rejection that seemed so personal at such a young age. I told myself I didn't care, and the common theme on my report cards became 'Belinda is wasting her potential' and I was. I wouldn't learn the real value of education until later in my life.

I left Broken Hill for Brisbane in 1994 at the age of twenty with Paul, to whom I was already married, and Dylan who was eighteen months old. Paul had been a miner and made redundant along with a lot of the other Broken Hill miners. We packed all our belongings into a trailer, having decided to start a new life for our young family in Queensland, the Sunshine State. Having grown up in a Catholic family, we married just after the birth of Dylan. I was only eighteen and Paul twenty-one. We didn't have much money so couldn't afford a reception, but our family and friends insisted we do something to celebrate so, after the ceremony at the cathedral, we all went to dinner at the local RSL. To balance out the institutionalised component of the wedding, I showed some 90s' flair, my youth and my rebellious nature by wearing a short wedding dress with a train. A rock music fan, I had modelled my dress on the one worn in the Guns N' Roses *November Rain* music video. We finished the evening at the local Night Train Disco, Broken Hill's 'premier nightclub and live music venue' but known to locals as the 'fight train', a reference to its place, in years gone by, on the NSW most violent venues list.

You see things through a clearer lens with age and in retrospect. I now realise that when I was growing up, the staunch unionism of the town informed some of my early years. It was illegal for married women to work in Broken Hill from 1930 until 1981. Although I had an inner yearning to work in the creative arts, I sidelined my dreams and ambitions to focus on marriage and motherhood. Fear had been a constant in my life since I had been the victim of domestic violence in my teenage years which caused me to withdraw in an attempt not to be seen.

Years before Dylan's accident, sitting inside a tiny plane strapped to a skydiver, I was determined to face one of my many fears: the fear of heights. I was wearing my Bon Jovi shirt for good luck and the ink was still fresh on the band's motivational lyrics – 'It's My Life' – I recently had tattooed on my foot, as beads of nervous sweat gathered on my forehead. But I was determined not to back down, as I had so many times in the preceding years, just because I was afraid. I was determined to feel the fear and do it anyway!

I remembered standing at the open door preparing to jump, a million conflicting emotions running through me. But also with a deep knowing that, if I didn't overcome my fear, I would spend my life sitting on the sidelines, watching others living by their passions, not having the courage to pursue my own.

As I prepared to jump, I recall looking around the plane at the faces of Dylan and Mikaela who looked as excited as I felt nervous. Hudson (ten at the time) was waiting on the beach with friends to watch our descent.

'Five, four, three, two, one.'

And just like that, we were out the door!

The cold air took my breath away, as did the thrill of free-falling to the earth at a rapid pace before my skydiver pulled the cord. Then the parachute turned our swift free-fall into the most peaceful descent. The freedom I felt in that moment was like nothing I had ever felt before. As we approached the beach, I saw Hudson sitting near the X waiting for us to land, which we did with precision.

Dylan and Mikaela landed in quick succession after me and we shared a moment of pure elation, the euphoria not being something I could put into words. I realised that I had missed many amazing experiences in my life due to being overcome by fear. Sitting beside my child in a coma would teach me that I never really knew what fear was until that moment, but I knew I must hold the vision of Dylan healing rather than allow myself to descend into fear.

I was thinking of this at the end of that first day in ICU, as I placed one hand on Dylan's head and the other on his heart and pictured the brightest ray of white light coming down from above and covering Dylan. I pictured him regaining his full health.

The young male nurse stationed in Dylan's cubicle gently interrupted my meditation to inform me it was time for Dylan to be turned again. He encouraged me to go home for the night and get some sleep.

'This is going to be a long journey,' he said, 'you need to pace yourself so you can go the distance.'

I agreed to leave the room but there was no way I was leaving the hospital.

In the waiting room, family, friends, and other visitors were packing up their belongings in preparation to leave for the night. Visiting hours had ended and everyone there for Dylan lined up to say goodnight to me and ask if there was anything I needed brought up the following day. I said goodnight to Miki last, but she said she wasn't leaving.

Her beautiful blue eyes were red and swollen from crying, her thick blonde hair tied loosely back from her tear-stained face; she looked as exhausted as I felt.

Although I wished she would go home to bed for her sake, if she felt she needed to be there, I was not going to stand in her way, and besides, I didn't want to be alone. I pulled a notepad out of the backpack I'd taken with me to Broken Hill and suggested that we write messages in it for Dylan to read when he woke up.

A couple who had been in and out of the waiting room all day, like us, had also decided to stay the night. With the crowds of people now gone, I could see every inch of the room. It was lined with multi-coloured carpet squares that, if you looked closely enough, didn't seem to line up. The walls were covered with medical posters and the small space was filled with various lounges and chairs. Miki and I pushed together a couple of teal two-seater vinyl lounges so we could snuggle up with Rachel's blanket, along with the pillows and blankets Frannie sent up earlier with my brother Mick who works at the Princess Alexandra (PA) Hospital. Mick had been there overnight in my absence, alongside Paul and Miki. I wrapped my arms around my daughter who, despite her maturity, was still the little girl who thought my kisses could make everything better. I told her how proud I was of her, of her strength over the last twenty-four hours.

'I love you mum,' she said.

'Love you too, toots.'

Thursday 15th, March 2012 - Day 2

My Dearest Dylan,

From the moment I found out about the accident, I asked the angels to protect you and sent you love and light. Seeing you hooked up to all the machines and tubes was hard but at least I am finally with you my beautiful boy and I will not leave your side until you are 100% better. So many people are sending messages of love and well wishes and others are praying for you. I know these prayers will be answered as you are a beautiful soul with so much more to do here on earth, and anyway, I am not letting you go anywhere. I love you with all my heart! Mumma XX

CHAPTER THREE

Is it Better to Give False Hope or False Despair?

I woke up hoping it had all been a terrible nightmare, which it was, of course, but the kind you have when you are awake. I looked over at Miki who was still fast asleep and got up quietly so as not to wake her.

In the ICU, the same kind nurse from the night before informed me there had been no change overnight and that the doctors would give me a more in-depth update after their rounds, later that morning.

I gave Dylan a kiss good morning. Seeing him lying there so vulnerable reminded me of when he was a baby. I would sing him to sleep, wanting the words to protect him from all the bad things in the world. Being a mad Bon Jovi fan my entire life, I often sang the kids Bon Jovi songs rather than nursery rhymes, to the amusement of my family and friends. Music has a way of reaching you when nothing else can. Most of the memories and moments of my life have been played out to a Bon Jovi soundtrack. Their lyrics got me through some of my greatest challenges, and I now faced my greatest challenge yet.

Dylan began to cough so I picked up a tissue from the desk and wiped the drool from the side of his mouth, being extra careful not to touch the ventilator tube. I wondered what horrific images Hudson must have seen in his google search and what he would be imagining about what his brother looked like.

I decided to take a photo of Dylan so I could show Hudson exactly what he looked like in the ICU. I can't quite explain why but taking a photo of Dylan in this vulnerable state felt wrong to me; it would be the one and only photo I ever took of Dylan in a coma.

I sent the picture off to Frannie so that she could show Hudson what he could expect to see if he came to visit his brother in the ICU. Hudson had looked up to his big brother since the moment he was born, and I believed Dylan needed to hear his voice along with the rest of his family. Having to make so many important decisions that would impact on my children's lives weighed heavily on me. All I could do was follow my inner compass, but one thing had already become clear, a level of childhood innocence was going to be lost along the way for both Mikaela and Hudson.

Later that second day, Hudson came to the hospital with Frannie. It had only been a couple of days since I had seen them but it felt like a lifetime. Hudson raced into my arms. When Frannie joined us I saw her pain and concern and knew that the horror I was feeling was also felt by her.

Dylan's lifelong best mates Chris and Nathanial arrived later, and numerous other friends and family. Some brought meals they had graciously prepared, for which we were extremely grateful.

The empty waiting room had once again become a bustling hub of activity.

I gently escorted Hudson down the long hallway to see his big brother. As we approached Dylan's bed, the ICU nurse got up from his stool and reached out a hand to Hudson.

'Hey champ,' he said, 'you must be Dylan's little brother. I bet he's going to be happy that you're here.'

'Hey Dylan,' Hudson said, the emotion making his voice quiver, 'we're making you a poster, and there's lots of people here waiting for you to wake up. You have to wake up, Dylan.'

Hudson asked if he could return to the waiting room.

It was hard to believe that just a few nights ago I was looking at Dylan and Hudson sitting on the back of Dylan's new Ute outside Baskin and Robbins eating ice cream and laughing. I distinctly remember thinking how much the brothers loved and adored each other, what I would give to hear them laughing together now. My phone had been ringing consistently for days. I appreciated everyone's calls, but I needed to conserve my energy. Still, when I saw a call coming in from my dear friend Kerry, I knew I had to take it.

Kerry is a physiotherapist who has worked in brain injury rehabilitation and was, incredibly, at a brain injury conference as we spoke. She told me not to give up hope, that she had seen so many people come out of their coma and recover. She insisted I keep trying to reach Dylan, that he could hear me.

Later that day we were invited to meet with a doctor for an update on Dylan's condition.

He explained that Dylan had sustained a traumatic brain injury caused by scattered lesions over a widespread area of the brain, as well as bruising and bleeding in the brain. He also had fractures in his spine and ribs, a collapsed lung, and a penetrating elbow wound. He explained there was no way to know if the damage to his brain would be permanent and that all we could do was wait for the swelling to go down before they could try to cut Dylan's medication back and bring him out of his medically induced coma.

I looked across the table at my mum and Paul, their faces mirroring exactly what I was feeling: hopeless and helpless. Later, sitting by Dylan's bedside, I thought about how he was always the prankster, always making us laugh. Only a few months earlier I had been hospitalised with deep vein thrombosis, and Dylan, always the stirrer, was sitting beside me keeping me entertained, playing with the controls on the side of the bed making it go up and down, changing the television channel with his phone and giving me stick for wearing the sexy compression socks the hospital had given me. He was determined to keep my spirits up while we waited for the results of my CAT scan to see if my blood clot had moved from my leg to somewhere more sinister.

I now needed to be that for him. Rather than hope, I decided I was going to have complete faith that he would make a full recovery and knew that we must keep his spirits up and talk to him like we always had. If all he heard was people talking about how dire his condition was, he may not fight to return to us. I started giving him curry, just like he had done to me.

'Oh, look who's wearing a pair of those sexy socks now hey?' I teased. 'And you had to go one better and get yourself a pair of moon boots to go with them.'

Days passed. I finally convinced Miki she had to start going home at night, to sleep in her own bed. Everyone tried to convince me to do the same, but I wasn't budging, and neither was Doris, with whom I'd shared the waiting room from that very first night.

Doris also had a son in the ICU, Nathan. Nathan was a few years older than Dylan and coincidentally worked as a heavy diesel mechanic at the same company Dylan used to work for when he was doing his apprenticeship. Nathan had been coward-punched while out celebrating his buck's night. We always hear how one punch can kill, but not about how, sometimes, one punch can leave a person with lifelong brain damage. Or about the ripple effect of trauma this will have on the whole family.

Doris and I became sisters; mothers bonded by shared pain and fear, but also by hope, faith and determination. We vowed that both our boys would receive a miracle, and that we would do everything in our power to make sure they didn't just survive, but go on to thrive, living full lives filled with all the rich experiences they deserved.

As morning broke on day four, Doris and I packed up our bedding just as the waiting room filled with people. Miki arrived, proudly showing me some wool and knitting needles she had purchased so she could knit Dylan a beanie. She had recently passed her driving test so was able to drive Frannie and Hudson to the hospital every day. Huddo had just started high school at Aviation High, a long commute from our home, but he dreamed of being a pilot. It occurred to me that both he and Miki had not been to school since the accident happened, which was not ideal. Both were in pivotal years of their education: Hudson in his first year of high school and Miki in her last.

It was Saturday so we had extra visitors, including my Broken Hill tribe, ever present during this time. There were a lot of ex-Broken Hillians in Queensland and we all seemed to gravitate towards one another. I had known Kerri-Lee and Kyla since my childhood, and Kerri-Lee was my longest-standing and dearest friend. We met at the grand old age of six, when I moved into the house next door to her.

Our continuing bond was now rooted in the deep spiritual journey we had both undertaken in recent years, attending meditation together on Monday nights under the guidance of the beautiful Roxanne. Kyla and I had reconnected a few years earlier having both gone through marriage break-ups at the same time, we had been each other's rock throughout the difficult times and shared many adventures and laughs as we rediscovered single life and dating in our thirties. Caroline, also from Broken Hill, was a new connection for me but it felt like we had known each other forever. All three of these amazing women were a huge support to me during this time as were many others who supported us from both near and far, including my mum, dad and brother, as well as Paul's parents, Jenny and Darryl, who had flown to Brisbane to be by Paul's side. The waiting room was always a hive of activity, and it was overwhelming at times. I nominated spokespeople from different groups of family and friends so they could pass on updates about Dylan because having to respond to everyone became too taxing on me personally.

The outpouring of love and support we experienced was heartwarming. We had donations of money, gift cards, meals and my workplace even bought me a parking pass. These gifts eased the financial strain we were under with no income for the foreseeable future. Money isn't something I had thought about, or wanted to for that matter, but the reality was that I had a mortgage to pay, and I worked as a casual at a law firm which meant I didn't have any sick pay or holiday entitlements.

On Day 4 the doctors informed us they were going to cut back Dylan's medication to see how he would respond. I was excited and afraid. Would Dylan remember us? To even consider that he wouldn't was too horrible a thought to bear.

I turned Dylan's ring with my fingers, as I had been wearing it on my necklace so I could feel close to him. This suddenly gave me the idea to take the crystal off my necklace and place it in a drawstring bag beside Dylan so he could feel my energy with him all the time. What followed was a touching display of love for Dylan. Everyone started removing pieces of jewellery and adding it to the bag. These were valuable, personal items, and I truly felt the collective energy and knew that Dylan would also.

Tokens in hand, I re-entered the ICU. Dylan's bed came into view and I witnessed him open his eyes, stand up, and begin pulling all his tubes out. He was highly agitated and looked terrified. I was about to run to him but was blocked by nurses and wardies running from every direction.

With a million thoughts running through my head I was asked to go back to the waiting room. He must have felt so scared waking up with a tube down his throat, all those wires and cords coming out of him, and completely naked except for a small blanket to cover him.

In the waiting room I filled everyone in on what was happening and, again, waited for that stupid phone on the wall to ring!

Tick, tock, tick, tock, always watching the damn clock, fears in my head that just won't stop.

When I was finally allowed to go back in the ICU, Dylan had been re-sedated. I couldn't stop the silent tears as a rollercoaster of emotions caught up with me. I took Dylan's hand and tried to reassure him everything was going to be okay. I was probably trying to reassure myself also.

'You are one stubborn and determined young man, Dylan Adams,' I said. 'Did you think you were going to just get up and walk straight out of here! I know you must be frightened, but we really need you to be calm, mate, but still keep fighting. I know you can make your way back to us!'

Saturday 17th, March 2012 - Day 4

Dear Dylan,

I hope when you do wake up next time, you are not as scared, but I can totally understand why you would be. All the doctors and nurses are taking really good care of you, and we are getting so many people ringing and messaging to wish you a speedy recovery. You have a collection of people's special things so you can feel all our positive, loving energy for you, and I have been wearing your ring so I can feel your energy with me. I have been asking the universe, angels, God, and even our loved ones that have passed to please help heal you. I have been here at the hospital every day and night, seeing you in this vulnerable state breaks my heart but I know you are going to make a full recovery because you are a fighter, you are my son so of course you are a fighter. I will do everything I can to see you make a full recovery and live the life you deserve, rich with love, friendship, and good health.

Love you to the stars and back times a million.

Love Mumma X

As I sat beside Dylan early one morning, I found myself wondering what day it was. They all seemed to blur together now. I valued the quiet alone time I had with Dylan in the mornings before all the other visitors arrived, or alone as we could be with the hustle and bustle of the medical staff carrying out lifesaving tasks around us.

The limited visitation times and two-person rule meant time with Dylan was always brief. I had become very protective of him in his vulnerable state and limited his visitors to immediate family, grandparents, aunties, uncles, and cousins. I encouraged everyone to keep the atmosphere positive when visiting; not an easy task when seeing Dylan hooked up to life support, which would naturally cause overwhelming feelings of deep sadness and fear, but I didn't want those emotions passed on to Dylan. When I found myself slipping in that direction, I would leave his bedside and go outside for a chat with someone or for a cry if needed.

My sudden strength during that time surprised everyone, mostly myself. I had always sat outside in the waiting room while Paul took the kids in for their needles as I couldn't stand to see anyone in pain, especially my babies. I was grateful that the past two years, post-divorce, had trained me to face fear head-on, though nothing could ever prepare you to face the prospect of your child dying. Still, the hardships had built my resilience, given me a strength I didn't have just a few short years earlier. And I needed every bit of strength I could muster.

Later that morning, after the doctors' rounds, we were given the news that Dylan had developed pneumonia. He was now to be kept in the medically induced coma until the pneumonia healed. Dylan's condition was now more dire than it had been just days earlier.

I was also informed that I must begin going home at night and would no longer be allowed to sleep in the waiting room. I was told I had a long journey ahead and needed to try to get some decent sleep if I was going to last the distance. I hadn't had a decent sleep since the accident and didn't think going home to my own bed was going to change that, but I couldn't continue to sleep in the waiting room long-term, and it was now clear that it was a long-term situation we were dealing with.

Day turned to night again. I went home for the first time since I had left for Broken Hill five days earlier. Five days that felt like an eternity. I was overwhelmingly afraid. What if something happened to Dylan and I wouldn't be there or make it back in time.

As I crawled into bed, I listened for the familiar sound of Dylan's car pulling into the driveway and the electric roller door going up. I would always get annoyed at the bass thumping so loud on his stereo that I could hear him from around the corner, but boy would I have given anything to hear that sound as I tucked myself into the foetal position and eventually cried myself to sleep.

Three more days passed. It was now Day 8, with still no change. The more time that passes, the harder it is not to allow yourself to slip into complete hopelessness, especially when you hear stories of people being in a coma for months, even years. The only thing I could control was my own inner narrative, so I began writing affirmations in my diary every single day.

Dylan will open his eyes and wake up calmly! He will know who we are and will make a full recovery. Mikaela and Hudson had still not returned to school. I was concerned about the effect this would have on their education, but I knew that they were not in a place emotionally to be able to attend. I couldn't expect them to carry on as normal when our whole world had turned upside down. I couldn't, so I had no right to expect them to.

The ICU waiting room had now become a sea of knitters, thanks to Miki and her beanie. Everyone needed to feel useful, and the days passed so slowly there. Doris and I refer to the ICU as a private club you never want to belong to. The long days wear you down emotionally. For that very reason I only had Hudson visit for brief periods each day, with Frannie or Paul.

We rolled into week two. An appointment had been organised for me to sit with a social worker at the hospital to try to sort out our finances. I now had zero income. This would be the first time I realised just how fucked our system is. I was informed that the only option for myself and Dylan was to apply for Newstart, a jobseeker payment.

'Wouldn't we apply for disability payment for Dylan and carer payment for myself?' I asked.

Apparently being in a coma hooked up to life support machines with a traumatic brain injury that would have lifelong effects – should he ever make it out – didn't meet the criteria for a disability payment. It wasn't classed as permanent.

So Dylan is in a coma with a severe traumatic brain injury that is going to affect him for the rest of his life IF he wakes up, but he doesn't have a disability and is going to be a jobseeker? How the fuck is he supposed to look for work? And, as for me, I have a job that I am unable to attend presently because I am here providing care for my son!

To top it off, because Dylan was nineteen at the time, I was unable to speak on his behalf to deal with any of his financial, medical or legal affairs without becoming his legal guardian and administrator. To do this I must apply to QCAT (Queensland Civil Administrative Tribunal) and attend a hearing so they could determine if I was fit to handle Dylan's affairs. I imagine there are a lot of unscrupulous people in the world who take advantage of the vulnerable, but I was already running on empty, so dealing with bureaucratic red tape had my head spinning.

As I sat beside Dylan on Day 8, I called upon all the meditation knowledge I had. One hand on his heart, one on his head, I visualised white light streaming down into his body healing every single cell.

As another day drew to a close I sang-whispered a quiet chorus so familiar to him....

I'll be there for you, these five words I swear to you, when you breathe, I wanna be the air for you. I'll be there for you! I'd live and I'd die for you, I'd steal the sun from the sky for you, words can't say what love can do, I'll be there for you.

~ Bon Jovi

Day 9 Day 10 Day 11

Chapter Four

Do You Know Who I Am?

Twelve days had passed. I arrived at the hospital to the news we'd been longing to hear, Dylan had recovered from pneumonia. The doctors were finally going to begin reducing his sedation again and bring him out of the medically induced coma he had now been in for twelve days. It was over a week since the first attempt, and I was anxious that Dylan would wake up afraid and agitated again, clinging to all the hope I could muster that he would instead wake up calmly and remember who we were.

'Okay sleeping beauty,' I said, 'it's time to open those beautiful eyes of yours!'

I had been playing Dylan his favourite music for days, but it suddenly occurred to me that I had a video on my phone of Dylan's cat Max. Max was one of the many animals Dylan had rescued over the years, but the connection they shared was special. Max was one of those once-in-a-lifetime pets.

I played the video of Max meowing and told Dylan that Max was missing him and waiting for him to come home. As I sat down beside Dylan and took his hand in mine, I felt the gentlest squeeze and wondered if I had imagined it. It reminded me of when I was pregnant with him and felt the flutter of movement inside my tummy for the very first time.

'Can you hear me, Dylan? It's time to come back to us, my beautiful boy.'

Dylan raised his hand and touched my face. Tears of joy streamed down my face.

The ICU nurse suddenly appeared beside me.

'Keep talking to him, he's responding to you,' he said, just as Dylan opened his eyes.

'Hey you,' I said, 'it's about time we got a glimpse of those beautiful eyes of yours. I have missed seeing them.' Relief flooded my very being.

Dylan looked around, taking in his surroundings with an unmistakable look of confusion. He couldn't speak because he still had the breathing tube in his mouth. It was an exciting and terrifying moment. As he became more alert, he lifted his hand to the tube in his mouth. The nurse stepped forward and calmly said.

'Dylan, you are in the ICU, you have a tube in your mouth to help you breathe, okay.'

This was the glimmer of hope we had been praying for.

Monday 26th March, 2012 - Day 12

Dear Dylan,

Today was the best day since you have been here. The doctors cut back your sedation and you looked at me and responded to some of my questions by nodding your head and squeezing my hand. It was a very exciting moment. I can't wait until they take your breathing tube out and you can talk to us, this will hopefully be tomorrow. The doctors don't know yet if you will have memory loss or even some personality changes for a while because you still have bruising on your brain, but I KNOW you are going to be okay and back to yourself in no time. I stayed with you from first thing in the morning until late at night when they kick me out. The first week I slept in the waiting room but that was making the nurses cranky with me so now I do go home to sleep. I hope when you fully wake up, you forget the accident part. It must have been terrifying. I haven't been able to get Miki and Huddo to go to school, they want to be here with you. Everyone is so worried about you! Do you know, all my friends have been praying for you and sending you healing energy as have your friends who have been here every day. You are so loved and such a special boy, the amount of people wishing you well and wanting to help has been overwhelming. I have been meditating and sending you light every single day, you are going to be okay my beautiful, special boy! I love you!

Mumma XXX

Day 13 as the sun rose on a new day, I was filled with hope that they would be able to take Dylan's breathing tube out and he would finally be able to speak to us. We were all so relieved that this time he had woken up calm, although afraid and confused.

A lot of people were present and supportive during this time, and we would never have gotten through without the meals made and gift vouchers given. The parking pass purchased for me by my work colleagues at Merthyr Law had saved hundreds of dollars in parking fees. The cost of parking at the hospital is not cheap, especially when you are there all day every day, yet it is a necessity. All these gifts alleviated some of the stress I was under so I could focus where I needed to, on Dylan. I was overwhelmed with gratitude to my community of family, friends, and work colleagues because at times like these, it really does take a village.

Money issues weren't something I wanted to think about at an already stressful time, but the fact was, our budget was already tight as I was still adjusting to life after divorce. I had been working three days a week as an administration assistant whilst I completed my study and was trying to work my way into the film and television industry as a makeup artist, having only secured my first break the previous year with some additional days on PJ Hogan's *Mental* starring Tony Collete.

I had zero entitlements as far as paid leave went and, sadly, Dylan had left his apprenticeship to start his landscaping business a few months before his crash. He had no paid leave, and his superannuation personal injury insurance had expired weeks prior because he was self-employed and therefore hadn't continued to pay into his superannuation. We were dealt another blow when we were informed that Dylan couldn't claim for personal injury on his insurance because, at that time in Queensland, you were not entitled if you were 'at fault' and it was a single vehicle accident, so he was at fault.

The jobseeker payments we had begun receiving were less than $300 a week, and with that I was supposed to pay my mortgage, utilities, put fuel in my car and food on the table for my kids. I put our home loan repayments on hold for six months on compassionate grounds, which helped ease the burden, but the financial strain was extreme, and all these processes chipped away at my self-esteem and pride.

Dylan was becoming more aware and responding to questions with a nod or a squeeze, so they were finally ready to take out his breathing tube. I could not wait to hear his voice again. I felt hopeful that he would remember us, given that he was squeezing my hand and nodding in answer to questions.

We weren't allowed to be in the ICU while they removed all the life support machines. I was kind of relieved that I didn't have to witness them pulling that long tube out of Dylan's throat; there is only so much you can witness and continue to hold yourself together.

Later that morning I returned to the ICU with Mikaela by my side. We were overjoyed to see Dylan without all the machines hooked up to him. He still had a feeding tube and was now restrained by wrist ties to the bed. He was at a high risk of a fall which could result in further trauma to his brain. Because he was not mobile, he needed to wear a pad, this was one of the many reasons I had only allowed family to visit. I wanted to protect him while he was so vulnerable, until I could gauge to what capacity he could remember. I worried that too many people could be overwhelming and confusing for him.

Miki and I sat by Dylan's bedside.

'Do you know who I am?' Miki asked.

'Michael Jackson?' Dylan was always the prankster, so it was hard to know if he was joking with us now.

'No,' she said gently.

'George Bush, George Bush, W George Bush,' he said, then burst out laughing, repeatedly saying his own name. It was exciting to hear him speak for the first time in weeks but terrifying too. This was a very different boy to the one who said goodbye to me at the airport weeks earlier.

The ICU nurse explained to us that we may see some changes in Dylan's personality, trying to prepare us for the next steps of his recovery. He was being moved to the neuro ward, which meant he would be in a shared room and no longer have his own nurse. We were warned that this next phase is usually the most emotionally taxing on carers and family.

The wardies wheeled Dylan into his new room on the neuro ward, and some familiar faces greeted us. Dylan would be sharing a room with Nathan and two others. I was grateful, yet again, that I could share this next phase with Nathan's mum, Doris. We marvelled that both our boys had moved to the neuro ward the same day, so our shared membership in this exclusive club you never wanted to be part of continued to strengthen our bond. And now that our boys were awake, they would form a bond of their own.

Dylan slept on and off as the medications that had kept him in a coma slowly left his system. When he was awake, he was either staring off into space or talking incessantly. One day as he was watching the V8 supercars on TV he started making vroom vroom sounds. It was like he had reverted to childhood, except for his language and anger outbursts. One of these occurred when a nurse interrupted his V8 supercars to advise him that she needed to change his pad. Highly agitated, Dylan yelled:

'Fuck all your mothers, why don't you just pin my dick to the wall.'

Seeing the absolute horror on my face, the nurse took a moment to explain to me how brain injury often affects a person's inhibitions, telling me the aggression was normal.

It all sounded like just another day for her, but for me, well, it was breaking my heart. I could feel the walls closing in on me...

I felt a comforting arm around me and looked up to see that my pain was shared by my new friend Doris.

'How about we take a walk for a minute and get a coffee?' she said.

Doris gently steered me downstairs to Starbucks, which was located in the foyer of the hospital. It almost felt like we were just two friends meeting for a coffee date and was probably the most 'normal' moment I'd had in weeks.

'Well, they certainly don't wake up from a coma like that in the movies,' I said to Doris.

'Not any movie I've ever seen,' she agreed.

'Nathan seems a lot calmer than Dylan, I guess it's like they keep telling us, all brain injuries really are different, and everyone is affected in different ways.' I voiced my thoughts for the first time.

'It's still early days, we are both getting a miracle remember. Let's continue to hold on to that.' Doris said this with conviction, lending me her strength at a time when I'm sure she was struggling to find her own.

On Saturday mornings Paul took the early morning shift. It felt like such a luxury to have those extra hours to get some housework done and, most importantly of all, to have a long breakfast with Miki and Huddo and catch up on all that I was missing in their worlds.

Miki was super excited to get up to the hospital that Saturday to see Dylan, because she had finally completed the beanie, knitting love and compassion into every single stitch. In the ward, Dylan was wearing Paul's sunglasses. 'Looking pretty cool there Dylan,' I said.

'My name is Paul,' Dylan said.

'He demanded I give him my pants as well,' Paul said, trying to convince Dylan to return his sunglasses now that the kids and I had arrived. Dylan was allowed to have his arms unrestrained when someone was there to supervise him and make sure he didn't try to go anywhere. He was still at a high risk of a fall.

He'd clearly decided this was his chance to put on a disguise and leave. Paul finally retrieved his sunglasses and said goodbye. Miki pulled the beige slouch beanie out of her bag and handed it to Dylan.

'I knitted you a beanie, Dylan, it's stylish like the one David Beckham wears.'

'I love it, I think I'm going to cry.' He was suddenly overcome with emotion. I hoped we would experience more of this gentler side of Dylan than the confused and agitated Dylan we were greeted by that morning.

That evening, fatiguing, Dylan became agitated again and, in a moment of frustration, ripped off his new beanie, threw it onto the floor in disgust and declared, 'Stylish, this isn't stylish!'

I was thankful Miki was not there to see her masterpiece thrown to the floor.

Now that Dylan was out of the ICU and in the neuro ward, we all tried to get into a new version of a 'normal' routine. Miki and Huddo finally returned to school after two weeks of absences, Paul returned to work and so did Frannie. Frannie and I worked at the same law firm so she was covering my job while I was on extended leave without pay so they didn't get anyone else in to replace me.

Each day my dad, Gary, would do the 5 to 7 am shift, I would do the 7 am to 6 pm shift, Miki would visit every afternoon after school before returning home in time to look after Huddo when he got back from Aviation High late afternoon. Paul would relieve me at 6 pm and Frannie would relieve him at 7 pm, catching the bus straight from work to the hospital. One of us was always with Dylan from early morning until he went to sleep.

A physiotherapist and occupational therapist now visited Dylan every day. He was daily asked a series of questions to ascertain if he was suffering from PTA (post-traumatic amnesia), which he seemed to find especially tiresome. He was like a sponge, absorbing everything. If you told him something he would repeat it back to you. He would also repeat everything he heard on television, so we were careful to keep the channel on Discovery so at least he would be repeating things that were informative. 'Why do they keep asking me who the prime minister of Australia is,' he'd say to me. 'It's the same person it was yesterday.'

The next time he was asked that question he answered 'Belinda Adams' which gave us all a much-needed laugh.

Dylan talked incessantly during those four long weeks in the neuro ward; which can be a common deficit after a brain injury if there is damage to the frontal lobe. I have never heard anyone talk so much in my entire life. It was extremely exhausting, and I came to treasure the brief moments when Dylan would drift off to sleep, when I could hear myself think. I had waited weeks for him to wake up, and now I was treasuring the moments he was asleep! It gave me mother's guilt times a million.

I needed a mental escape from the clinical environment I was in all day, so I decided I would begin writing my first screenplay during those rare moments when Dylan slept. I'd had an idea floating around for a few years, a story about a girl growing up in a remote outback town who dreamed of being a singer. Inspired by the music of her favourite rock band, she finds the courage to follow her dreams. The working title would be 'Chasing Bon Jovi'.

The feeding tube in Dylan's nose was becoming a major source of irritation and discomfort. He refused to eat the pureed food, screwing up his nose and closing his mouth tightly. I asked if we could possibly try something else that was a similar texture, that he could swallow okay after having the tube down his throat, but they were only allowed to give patients specific foods in these early stages.

Dylan's frustration soon hit breaking point again, only this time instead of pulling a beanie off his head, he grabbed hold of his feeding tube and ripped it out. I will never forget him screaming in pain as they reinserted the tube.

That night, Dylan was restrained to the bed again. He thrashed around, trying to break free until he helplessly declared he wished he had died. I couldn't imagine how terrified he must have felt, strapped to a bed in a ward full of people who, due to their injuries, were also unable to move.

There will never be words to express how painful it was to witness this and, as his mum, to also sometimes bear the brunt of the most painful things said to me in his state of heightened fear and lessened inhibition. What little strength I had was slipping away. With tears streaming down my face I would tell myself, 'It's not Dylan, it's the brain injury'. Once a patient becomes agitated, they are given a sedative to calm them down. It was becoming clear that procedure was holding Dylan back. He was angry because he was restrained and wearing a nappy; he was restrained because he was at a high risk of a fall; he was at a high risk because he hadn't eaten food for weeks, and he refused to eat pureed fruit.

I crawled into bed that night worrying that if Dylan awoke in the night, he would feel frightened, trapped, scared and alone unable to move. I couldn't protect him from this no matter how much I wished I could.

My journals and my writing had become my best friend. I could say all the things I was feeling that couldn't be voiced.

When these four walls are all, you see,

I'll create a world for you and me.

I'll hold your hand; I'll share your pain.

I'll give you my strength and I'll hide my strain.

I'll hold you close, I'll wipe your tears,

I'll stay with you & take away your fears.

I love you deeper than the eyes can see,

Our souls are linked for eternity.

As time ticks on, and the world keeps turning,

I'll be right here keeping the fires of hope burning.

I'll never give up or leave you alone,

I will fight for you until I bring you home.

I'll find a strength like I've never known,

To fight for you until I bring you home.

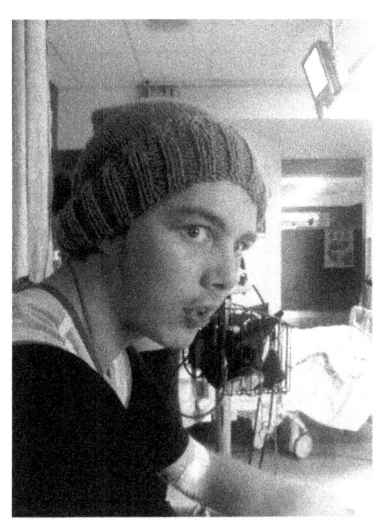

Dylan wearing his stylish beanie in the neuro ward

CHAPTER FIVE

Please Help

It was Easter Friday. Twenty-four days had passed since Dylan's accident, and for the next four days, which were a long weekend, Dylan wouldn't receive any therapy sessions.

I decided to take over. First, I was going to see if I could get him to eat and arrived at the hospital with a small tub of potato and gravy.

I pulled the curtain around his bed to give us some privacy and, nervously, scooped a small amount into his mouth. He didn't seem to have any issues swallowing, indicated he wanted more, and hungrily finished all the potato and gravy like it was the best thing he had ever tasted.

I continued for days, feeding Dylan potato and gravy, ice cream and yoghurt, until he ripped his feeding tube out again. I fessed up to the nurses that I had been feeding him and that he didn't need the feeding tube. As he began to eat his strength slowly returned. We were able to put the walking brace on, one of us either side to support him and get him moving more.

Days passed and Dylan was soon able to take himself to the bathroom and move around freely. It was a huge step forward for him to regain some independence. He'd still need to be restrained at night for a while longer, but he was progressing quickly.

As Dylan's physical recovery improved so too did his memory. Things were still a little jumbled, but he remembered who we were. It was like he was slowly progressing through the years of childhood all over again, starting with the emotional maturity of a toddler, and now progressing to that of a primary schooler. We celebrated every single milestone with him, just as we did when he was young.

Every morning Dylan would stand at the neuro ward window waiting to see me walk out of the car park and into the main hospital entrance. The wave he gave me was so big and excited that it became known as the Forest Gump wave. Some days he would have his slippers on the wrong feet and his boxer shorts on over his pants. He still had the teddy we had gifted him in the ICU.

One morning I arrived to find Dylan wearing an electric bracelet around his wrist. Doris was across the room next to Nathan. 'Nathan is wearing one too!' she said.

'Really? What are they for?'

'Last night Dylan asked Nathan to untie him,' said Doris. 'They tried to leave the ward; said they were going to the rooftop bar. Apparently, they thought they were on a cruise ship! So now those bracelets set off an alarm if they go past the neuro reception area.'

'Oh my god,' I said. 'Imagine if they had gotten out of the hospital in their current state, who knows where they could have ended up.'

We had a good laugh. Sometimes you must find what little humour you can to survive.

Dylan's own sense of humour was also back in full force, and often his jokes were at my expense. One day he walked me out to the reception area, happily waving me goodbye. It made me highly suspicious, since he was always upset when I left, even if only for ten minutes. I waved at him as I walked towards the lift. The alarm went off as I passed the reception area. I turned to see Dylan shouting:

'Nurse, nurse, quick, she's trying to escape!'

What the hell, how did I set off the alarm? I walked back towards Dylan, then noticed the bracelet was no longer on his wrist.

'Dylan,' I said, 'where is your bracelet?'

'I don't know,' he said innocently.

I checked my jacket pockets, then my handbag, and voila, there it was. I cracked up laughing and Dylan did too.

Later I found Dylan sitting on his bed holding the medical file that was always clipped to the end, tears in his eyes. I rushed to his bedside wondering what had happened.

'I didn't know I was a divorced alcoholic!'

'That's because you're not, you're only nineteen, you've never been married, and you are not an alcoholic,' I reassured him.

'It says so right here.' He pointed to the chart. I took the chart and examined the page he had been reading.

'My darling, this is an example page, it's just showing the nurses how to fill out the chart.'

I realised that he had no real concept of how long he had been in a coma.

Dylan was regaining physical strength, so I was granted permission to take him out of his ward for short periods as long as we stayed within the hospital grounds. I mapped out our days with activities to keep him stimulated and to try to boost his mental well-being. Being in a clinical environment all day wears you down mentally and can become depressing after long periods of time, along with the increased risk of infection.

My dad, Gary, Dylan's first visitor of the day, would catch a bus to the PA Hospital in the wee hours of the morning. He used to work at the hospital so upon arrival he'd take Dylan downstairs for a coffee with his old workmates. They'd gather around what they called the table of knowledge. This was valuable time which enabled me to spend the mornings with Miki and Hudson.

When I arrived later in the morning, our first daily outing would be to go down to the hospital foyer and pretend were in an airport lounge awaiting a flight to some exotic location. I hoped encouraging Dylan to think up scenarios would help him remember things, as well as stimulate his brain creatively.

'Where are we flying today?' I'd ask.

We would create a story, alias names, and a reason for our travel. Once we had our imagined world for the day, we'd head to the hospital Starbucks and order coffee under our alias names, imagining we were sitting in Starbucks at our imagined destination waiting for our order to be prepared. I lost track of how many times we thought they had forgotten our orders, when it was we who'd forgotten our alias names being called repeatedly by the baristas!

Mid-morning, we'd lie on the grass at the front of the hospital in the sun, breathing in the fresh air. I recall looking up at the clouds passing by, wondering if this would be our life now.

I'd been struggling, in the preceding years, with the knowledge that my kids were getting older and wouldn't need me as much. There can be real grieving that accompanies your children getting closer to flying the nest, and for me, this was compounded by being on my own.

I was still working my way through feelings of worthlessness and being discarded after giving so many years of my life to someone. I'd put up a wall whenever a man got close to me. Of course, there had been numerous drunken nights out and one-night stands, but I wouldn't give these men my name, number, or any information about me. One night I picked up a guy at the kebab stand on my way home and the following day I felt as cheap and nasty as the kebab I'd eaten. They say a hungry heart is willing to eat anything.

Becoming a married mother at eighteen, I'd never really had the time or opportunity to date, or explore who I am, and I was enjoying the freedom of being a single woman. So many parts of my life were out of my control that I took what little control I could of my personal life.

I'd adopt personas on nights out with friends: Fawn the surgical assistant and Hunter the stunt woman, and some more mischievous aliases like Officer Yvette Beaver and Misty Stains the cleaner. The rest is best left to one's imagination! But I loved creating a world where I felt in control, even if just for the night, and exploring my sexuality – something I never did in my youth.

My friends nicknamed me the runner because I always disappeared when my companions fell asleep, sneaking out to catch a taxi home. I was always the one leaving. No man was going to get close to me or my kids, who I would protect at all costs.

I recall looking at Dylan lying on the grass, shielding his eyes from the bright glare of the sun, gazing innocently up at the sky. I wondered what thoughts or memories were running though his mind, and I was struck with the realisation that my once fear that he didn't need me anymore had been replaced with the very real fear that he may need me to care for him for the rest of his life. Talk about perspective!

I wished with all my heart that Dylan would regain his independence and have the opportunity to experience all that life had to offer. Some days, lying there, it felt like we would never leave that place.

One day I decided to take Dylan across the road to the little shopping village and get his haircut. One side had been shaved when they put the shunt in, and the other side had grown quite long. He was overdue a cut, but I also thought it might be nice for Dylan to do something normal. He sat in the hairdresser's chair, shocked when he saw his own reflection in the mirror.

'Oh my god, I'm fucking bald!'

He was really seeing himself again, for the first-time post-accident. Not only did he have half his head shaved but was very thin and looked quite frail. It was extremely confronting for him. He perked up, however, when the young hairdresser asked him how he would like his haircut, enjoying the everyday interaction and being fussed over in a normal way.

Dylan's spirits seemed slightly uplifted, and he was proud of his new hairdo as we made our way back over the road to the hospital, but our little outing left him fatigued and, back in his ward, he needed an afternoon sleep.

On the 19th of April, 2012, Dylan was assessed as being ready to transfer to BIRU (Brain Injury Rehabilitation Unit), located in a small brick building in the hospital grounds that also houses the Geriatric Rehabilitation Unit. But there were no beds available in the unit, so he was placed on a waiting list along with many others from all over the state.

I learned that BIRU only had twenty-six beds in total and, with some patients requiring inpatient care for months or a year, the wait to get a bed could be quite lengthy. We had been told numerous times that the first six months were the most crucial time for recovery following a brain injury, so it was mind-boggling that Dylan must now wait to receive the rehabilitation he so desperately needed.

The standard of care Dylan received from clinicians and hospital staff during his time in the ICU and neuro wards was exemplary, but with the acute phase of care behind him it was clear that the Queensland medical system was underfunded and a mess.

The transition meant that I was allowed to take Dylan out of the hospital grounds for brief periods during the day, but I couldn't take him home. I tried once and he refused to leave. It took quite a lot of cajoling to get him back into the car. So, I would take him for short walks in the botanical gardens or to the local park so he could get some fresh air and gentle exercise.

I also took him to see my physiotherapist friend, Kerry, who specialised in brain injury recovery. She performed cranial work on Dylan and showed me some simple movements I could do with him daily that would help stimulate his brain and assist in his recovery. On one occasion as Dylan and I prepared to leave her clinic, she handed me a book called

The Brain That Changes Itself by Doctor Norman Doidge. The book, an international bestseller, was about the science behind neuroplasticity and how the brain can heal even after it has sustained extensive damage. It became my bible.

Two days after learning that Dylan was on a waiting list for BIRU I could not bring myself to get out of bed. I had no strength left. When I started crying I wondered if I would ever stop. I was exhausted in every way imaginable. I heard a gentle knock on my door, it opened a crack, and there was Miki.

'Are you okay mum?'

'I don't know what's wrong with me today, I just can't get myself together.' I was still crying. She pleaded with me to take a day off and offered to go to the hospital in my place. I conceded defeat. I was completely and utterly broken.

That day I had time to really think for the first time, and my anger about the clear gaps in our health system began to build. I decided to write a letter to our Health Minister, the Hon Lawrence Springborg.

Dear Hon Lawrence Springborg,

Please Help.

My 19-year-old son recently suffered a traumatic brain injury in a car accident and I am just realising how underfunded the rehabilitation centres for this type of injury are. My son has made a significant recovery and is now ready to move to BIRU at the Princess Alexandra Hospital only there are no beds available. He is currently occupying a bed in the neuro ward where he is struggling to get through each long day with only ten minutes each day in therapy.

It is also madness that he is occupying a bed that could be used by a (medically) far sicker patient just because they have nowhere to put him until a place comes up in rehab. To think that the Brain Injury Rehabilitation Unit only houses 26 patients and those patients come from hospitals all over the state is crazy. The first six months is the most significant time in the recovery after a brain injury and my son needs to be getting every chance now to move forward in his recovery so as to have the best possible outcome yet is sitting in limbo.

I have taken indefinite leave from my job (a casual position so no holiday or sick pay) to be with him all day and try to keep him occupied while he awaits a rehab place. There is no indication as to when this will be, it could be weeks or months. I have even enquired about him attending the rehabilitation unit during the day, so he is at least getting the help he needs but this is not an option.

It is beyond frustrating to watch your child stuck in the system and not getting the best chance at a full recovery due to lack of funding. It also frustrates the hospital staff as they are doing everything they can but, without more funding from the government to expand the centre, their hands are tied.

I have seen so many heart wrenching stories during my time in the ICU and neuro ward over the last month and the one thing I have learnt is that this could happen to anyone!! Car accidents, people falling off ladders, boating accidents, one guy was king hit by a troublemaker on his bucks' night. I am sure if such an injury was sustained by one of your own family members you would want them to have a chance at the best recovery possible.

PLEASE make funding for expanding the Brain Injury Rehabilitation Unit at the Princess Alexandra Hospital a reality and help these patients and their families. You have no idea how helpless it feels to watch your child not getting the help they so desperately need at such a critical time.

I look forward to your prompt response.

Kind regards,

Belinda Adams

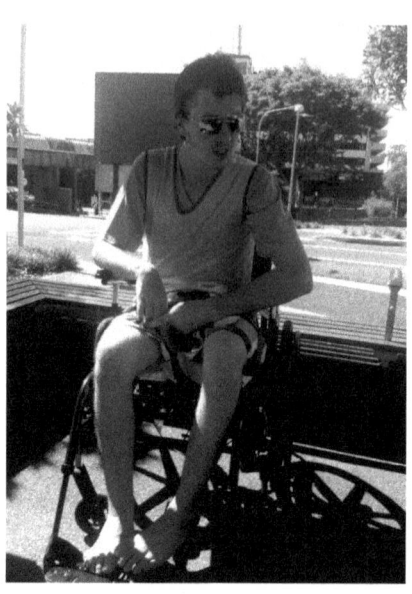

Dylan enjoying some time outdoors

Miki and Huddo taking their big brother for much needed time in the sun

Mum and son getting some fresh air

CHAPTER SIX

Mr Downey If You Please

After a weekend outing to the cinema to see the new Avengers movie, Dylan became completely fixated on Iron Man. He'd always had a passion for superheroes and, as a kid, he had been something of an inventor. He'd make robots and was interested in how things worked. He took up a diesel fitting apprenticeship at the age of fifteen so I could see why he felt a connection to the Tony Stark character, especially now. Stark was an inventor who built the Iron Man suit to protect himself when he was being held captive. He then used it to escape.

It wasn't just Iron Man that Dylan admired, he had also developed a hero worship for Robert Downey Jr., and decided he wanted to change his name officially to Dylan Downey. I asked him why Downey and not Tony Stark.

'Robert Downey Jr. went through a dark period in his life and a lot of people turned their back on him. He had to completely rebuild his life, and he came out of it stronger and more successful than ever. He is the real superhero!'

'Well, he may be yours, but you are definitely mine, Dylan Adams.'

'Dylan Downey,' he corrected, and all I could do was shake my head and giggle.

The day finally arrived for our hearing at QCAT (Queensland Civil Administrative Tribunal). I had applied for both myself and my mother Fran to become Dylan's legal guardians and administrators for financial, medical, and legal purposes. My mother had been my rock the preceding few months, my whole life really, and she stepped up again to help share this responsibility with me because I was too exhausted to do it all myself.

Mum takes care of everyone else before herself. Being one of seven kids growing up in a loving working-class family with a Catholic education in the mining town of Broken Hill, I imagine her options felt even more limited than mine did twenty years later. I know there were a few occasions in her childhood when she had to board away from home, when Grandma Addie was away for health-related reasons.

Her dad, Michael, a miner, couldn't take time off work to care for all seven kids on his own, so she had to stay at the convent and the Home of Compassion numerous times before she reached her teenage years. The Home of Compassion was like an orphanage for young girls up to sixteen years and an aged care nursing home run by the nuns. I recall her once telling me how she had many chores to do and had vivid memories of hanging out the wet washing on cold winter mornings feeling like her little fingers might snap off.

Her early teenage years were filled with odd jobs around the neighbourhood, like watering people's gardens, feeding pets and babysitting on Saturday nights. She began working at a chemist when she was sixteen.

Mum was also only sixteen when she met and married my father, Gary, after becoming pregnant with my brother. She became a wife and mother before she was even legally old enough to go to a pub. I came along just two years later and, like mine, mum's last birth was a traumatic one. She contracted septicemia and was deathly ill for weeks following my birth. Her compromised immune system never fully recovered, and she was diagnosed with an autoimmune condition that attacked her hips. Both hips were replaced in her early twenties, which is practically unheard of and much more common later in life. She had now had her hips replaced three times each, yet I never once heard her complain about the pain she must have been dealing with throughout her whole life. She has the same strength and grace as her mother before her.

My father grew up in a household of all boys: seven to be precise. There were times throughout my childhood when I felt he didn't know how to relate to me, especially in my teenage years. But I have fond memories of hot summer nights spent outside sleeping under the stars. He taught me to drive when I was fourteen, on the dirt country roads outside Broken Hill. He'd laugh as I bunny-hopped the car, taking off in first gear. As the years have passed our bond has grown and he never misses an opportunity to tell me how proud he is of his family.

It struck me, the day of the QCAT hearing, that how we view our parents changes. First, we look to them as these perfect superheroes who can do anything, followed by a more critical view as we become young adults and are finding our own identity and distancing ourselves. We finally reach a realisation that they too are human and have dealt with their own trauma, which they protected us from, only wanting us to see their strength and joy.

I wasn't sure what to expect at the QCAT hearing. It was basically a series of questions from a representative about Dylan's cognitive deficits post-accident, followed by a series of questions to determine our suitability to take legal responsibility for him.

Towards the end of the session, the representative asked Dylan if he had anything he would like to say.

'Yes, yes I do!'

I shuddered. A million thoughts ran around my head. What exactly was he going to say? I had a vision of Dylan declaring himself to be Iron Man, like the character did at the press conference at the end of the first Iron Man film.

'Stand up young man, what do you want to say?'

Dylan stood up confidently. 'I'd like to change my name.'

'What would you like to change your name to?'

'Dylan Downey.'

'Why would you like to change your last name to Downey?'

'Because Robert Downey hit rock bottom and now, he's better than ever!'

I felt like I was in a movie scene. Nothing could have prepared me for her response.

'If Dylan wants to change his last name, he has every right to,' she announced, then approved our application for administrators and guardianship. My mother and I exchanged a look of disbelief, wondering how someone could be seen to be lacking capacity to make legal decisions yet be allowed to change their last name. What if, as his recovery progresses, he regrets having changed his name whilst recovering from traumatic brain injury?

Dylan seemed to be standing ten feet tall with pride.

'See, I told you it was alright for me to change my name to Downey!'

'Okay Mr. Downey let's get you back to the hospital.'

I was unsure how I was going to manage the latest plot twist, and decided it was going to be a problem for later!

When I described the day's events to Doris, we laughed about the absurdity of the situation. What was most pressing for us both, though, was the rehabilitation issue. Our boys were both 'bed blocking', meaning someone is occupying a hospital bed due to a shortage of care elsewhere. Again, we had found ourselves, and our sons, in the same situation at the same time.

Doris had been looking at private rehabilitation options and had rung every rehab specialist in Brisbane to see if she could find a spot for Nathan. A receptionist took pity on her after hearing her story and gave them an immediate appointment for Nathan, instead of the normal six to nine months on the waiting list. Nathan now had a place in a four-week program at St Vincent's hospital. I was ecstatic for Nathan and Doris. It's impossible to adequately describe the bond Doris and I formed through the experience of almost losing our sons and the fight for rehabilitation. Something that should be a right, not a privilege.

This news led me to reassess our own rehabilitation options. Maybe I could plead to get Dylan into this program too, but we didn't have the finances, or insurance. It was one of the many things I couldn't afford. I was barely making ends meet post-divorce. Maybe I could sell my car? But that would take time we didn't have. The clock was ticking. Dylan needed rehabilitation, and he needed it immediately.

The strain of being Dylan's main source of companionship and therapy was weighing on me. I had less resilience for the moments when his frustration boiled over into angry outbursts.

My own anger reached the breaking point one day. I confronted one of the doctors doing his rounds, demanding to know when Dylan would be moving to rehab. He was unable to answer. I yelled.

'Do you have any idea what it is like to spend all day with a brain-injured person? I am not a therapist!'

It was not my finest moment. I was ashamed and horrified by my words, but I was running on empty and had reached a level of exhaustion that I had never known, in every respect.

Then the bed-blocking situation reached a new level of 'our system is fucked'. I arrived at the hospital one morning, but Dylan was no longer in the neuro ward. I was filled with hope. Maybe he had finally been given a place in BIRU? I soon learned that the bed he was in in the neuro ward was now needed by another patient, and because there was no bed available for him in BIRU, he had been moved to wherever a bed was available.

This would become our new normal. Where would I find Dylan each morning? It also meant that Dylan wasn't receiving any therapy, and his state of mind was declining. All he wanted was to come home, which he knew was the next step after BIRU.

I would later uncover numerous academic papers that backed up the experience we were having: there was a chronic lack of funding and rehabilitation options for people with brain injury. I knew of a patient, the same age as Dylan, who was being moved to an aged care facility. My heart broke a little more every day, from the collective pain of all the people we met on the devastating journey that is brain injury.

On the afternoon of Friday the 4th of May, 2012, Dylan and I returned to the ward (surgical I believe) he was in on that day to hear the news that Dylan was moving to a bed at BIRU! He'd now been in limbo for sixteen days, taking up space in acute care wards and not receiving the specialised rehabilitation he needed.

Dylan was excited, which is an understatement. He knew this was the final step of his inpatient care before being able to return home with us. It also meant I could return to work because visitors were not allowed until mid-afternoon in rehab. Dylan would now be able to come home on weekends because patients were given permission to go home Friday afternoons and return Monday mornings.

We packed up Dylan's things and moved across to BIRU. While Dylan was setting up in his new room, I spoke to the doctor at the front desk about taking Dylan home for the weekend, since it was Friday. 'Dylan isn't actually a patient of BIRU and if you take him home, you will be going against hospital policy.'

'What do you mean he is not a patient? We were just told he had a bed here?'

'A patient left today, and the next patient isn't due in here until Monday. They have moved Dylan over here for the weekend because there is a bed available.'

I could not believe this wasn't explained to us earlier. Dylan believed he finally had a bed in rehab. There was no way I'd get him back to the hospital now; besides they had nowhere to put him!

'Who do I speak to about this? I'm not moving him again.'

'You need to see the neuro doctors; he is still technically their patient.'

My head was spinning. I could feel my pulse thumping in my neck. What the actual fuck!

I collected Dylan from 'his room', and we went over to neuro reception. I told one of the nurses that we had been misled – that Dylan wasn't actually a patient; he was just an outlier there until Monday. I insisted Dylan would not be moving again and requested weekend release or this could be an interesting discussion for breakfast morning radio Monday morning.

The nurse asked us to take a seat while she sorted it out. I remember feeling angrier than I had ever felt in my entire life, but underneath that anger was a visceral fear. My son, scared and vulnerable beside me, had his whole life ahead of him and might not get the help he needed.

The nurse returned and advised us that the situation had been sorted. Back we went to BIRU. I was elated for Dylan but wondered if this meant someone else in desperate need of that place was going to miss out.

With Dylan finally in rehab and me working, we had money coming in again. It was nice to have a little normality return to our lives. Dylan's days were filled with much needed therapy, which included time with a speech therapist, occupational therapist, and physiotherapist. He was being taught about handling finances, learning to cook and did various craft activities. Time seemed to speed up again now that we were not sitting around waiting while life passed us by. Six weeks passed, and Dylan was finally able to return home.

It was a vision I had held onto from the very first moments I was informed of his accident. Something that seemed may never be possible in those early days. I was filled with gratitude, and a degree of concern. Dylan would be home alone while I was at work and the kids at school. Until that moment he had been in a locked ward for his own safety, and was still exhibiting challenging behaviours when neurofatigue set in. It was like all the information he had retained was scrambled. He just needed help to connect those dots again.

Dylan became frustrated with himself when he couldn't remember how to do things that had come easily prior to his accident. Sometimes in these moments of overwhelm he would say hurtful things to me. I knew it was Dylan's head injury, not him, and he would be overwhelmed with sadness and remorse afterwards, which pierced at my heart like tiny shards of glass.

I developed a thick skin and didn't take anything personally, but it was hard to be strong when my heart was breaking. Dylan was battling with feelings of loss of self, which accompanied his personality changes, and overwhelming feelings of isolation as he watched us get on with our lives while his stood still.

I worked three days a week and dedicated the other two to Dylan. He would still visit BIRU as an outpatient for a while, but other than that it was up to us to fill the time and work out strategies for his rehabilitation at home. I continued to read any book I could get my hands on about neuroplasticity and healing from brain trauma. We were amongst the lucky ones, to have Dylan recover to the degree he had already, but he had a long way to go to regain his independence. Lucky is a term that gets thrown about a lot at times like these; well-meaning people love to tell you how lucky you are that your child has survived and, believe me, we were. But having been through the hell of seeing my adult child go through a major trauma, become a shadow of his former self, lose his independence, ability to work, drive, and most of all lose himself to some degree, didn't feel lucky.

One afternoon as Miki and I pulled into the driveway, we discovered Dylan dancing around a drum, a fire burning inside it. He was singing.

'Burn baby burn.'

We jumped quickly out of the car, then to our horror, witnessed Dylan pick up a fuel container and pour it into the drum. A big fireball lapped at the roof of the shed. I grabbed the backyard hose and doused the flames.

'Dylan, what are you doing?'

'Burning the past and things from the people who have disappeared from my life.'

'Darling, you could have hurt yourself and burned the shed down, the drum is right under the veranda.'

'Yeah, well it needed to go.'

Miki whispered in my ear.

'Well, he's not wrong and you're the one who always says a full moon is a good time to burn and release stuff you want to let go of. Isn't it a full moon tonight?'

No words, just no words!

That night as I said goodnight to Hudson, I sent a grateful thank you to the universe that he had not been home to witness the fire incident. I could see he was traumatised by the changes in his brother. He was only twelve years old and, overnight, he essentially went from being the little brother to the big brother. Not to mention my lack of presence and attention. Hudson had always been an outgoing kid. He was extremely active and loved sports. He had played basketball and AFL throughout primary school and even took up ice skating for a while when he wanted to be a mighty duck. The preceding years had been difficult for him with the divorce, and now Dylan's accident to deal with at such an impressionable age.

Dylan was starting to get restless but was not cleared to drive again so could not return to his new landscaping business. He'd have to wait at least twelve months before the doctors would even consider letting him drive again, and then he would have to undertake specialised driver training with an occupational therapist and go through some serious testing before being declared competent.

Dylan's ongoing battle with fatigue made me think that a return to labouring in the heat was not going to be right for him now. I mentioned this to Doris during one of our regular catch-up calls. She contacted me not long after. She had organised for Dylan to do a few hours a day, a couple of days a week, at her office at Southbank. Dylan was thrilled to work again, but the office environment was completely new to him. He would catch the bus with me in the morning and get off at Southbank, then I'd meet him mid-afternoon when he finished work and we would bus home again. He would relay all the day's events excitedly to me on our way home. Sometimes people gave us strange looks because the volume of Dylan's voice would rise along with his excitement.

Dylan's favourite job was sorting and delivering the mail internally, and I think he spent a lot of time talking to people, still in his extremely talkative phase. Unfortunately, that job didn't last long. He wasn't quite ready to return to the workforce. With time on his hands, Dylan immersed himself deeper into the Iron Man fan world. Not only had he begun dressing like Tony Stark but started modelling his facial hair on the character.

In rare moments alone I escaped to another world, writing my screenplay. I was determined to write and produce my first feature film. I had a new outlook on life after the near death of my son and realised that all we have is *now* so we have to go after the life we dream of. I was following my heart instead of my head.

I approached my dear friend and ex–makeup teacher, Paige, to see if she would be interested in becoming my production partner to work with me to try to bring this film to life. Paige is one of those once-in-a-lifetime teachers who helps bring out the best in every single student, going above and beyond to help them reach their potential. She has been instrumental in the rise of so many makeup artists' careers. She was a huge support, both professionally and personally, at this time. Paige said she'd think about my proposal and encouraged me to keep going. I began attending writers' events and workshops and made the decision that I was not going to return to doing makeup. I enjoyed the experience, and meeting the people I did, but it never really felt like it was the right fit. I decided to focus on learning the art of screenwriting.

Mr Downey if you please

CHAPTER SEVEN

Life as Lyrics

I was running on empty. I needed time to myself to absorb everything that had happened. I also needed to complete my earlier, ill-fated trip to Broken Hill so I wouldn't carry an emotional block about leaving my kids for the rest of my life.

Mum stepped in to help, giving me peace of mind and the space to breathe for a moment.

At Adelaide airport, waiting for my flight to Broken Hill, it was impossible not to relive my previous journey five months earlier. I was deep in thought when I heard my phone buzzing with a message. Dylan was messaging me the image of three beautiful owls sitting on the fence in our backyard. A feeling of calm came over me, and a deep knowledge that all three of my kids were being looked after in my absence.

Owls had appeared often in my life, especially in the preceding few years as I delved into meditation and studied our connection to the earth and all living things. The more I learned, the more I noticed signs all around me, which I had come to believe were always there, I just hadn't been aware enough to see them. I think we have become so busy and disconnected that we often don't see what is right in front of us.

An owl had made itself at home in our backyard overlooking Dylan's room in the week leading up to his accident. This gave me a sense of protection. Dylan's accident had been a terrible tragedy, but there had also been synchronicities at play. He was still here with us, recovering, when the outcome could have been catastrophic.

I wanted to cram in all my favourite Broken Hill destinations on my brief stay. My first stop was Reganovich's for some of their famous hot chips and the best chicken salt in the country. I don't know one ex–Broken Hillian who doesn't make a visit to Reganovich's on their visits home. It's an essential stop.

The Palace Hotel is another iconic location made famous in the 1994 hit film *Priscilla Queen of the Desert*. The legendary muralled walls of the Palace Hotel were painted by Indigenous artist Gordon Waye in the 1980s. Then there's Bells Milk Bar and too many pubs to name. A pub crawl in Broken Hill really had you crawling, even before you made it from the northern end, at the Tydvil, to the main drag of Argent Street.

All these iconic locations were being weaved into my screenplay 'Chasing Jon', making Broken Hill itself a living, breathing character.

Broken Hill has a famously rich mining history and a vibrant arts scene. It was of course the home of Pro Hart.

For me another local icon is my Uncle Dolly. Every taxi home after a night out would have Uncle Dolly behind the wheel. Broken Hill is small, but it's not that small, so this become a running joke with family and friends.

I spent the next few days wrapped in love by family and friends. As I made the rounds, I realised that it was these very people whose support had kept us going just months earlier. For this I would be eternally grateful.

I was super excited to meet my new nephew Levi and give Bek a much-needed hug. Despite her years of nursing experience, I couldn't imagine how difficult it was for her, on that fateful day, to give me the news she did. She had gone into premature labour a week later and had to be flown to Adelaide by the Royal Flying Doctor Service and I wondered if the added stress had been a contributing factor. Thankfully the medical team in Adelaide had been able to stop the labour and Bek was able to return home where she eventually delivered another beautiful and healthy son.

I stayed with my lifelong friend Dean and his kids, Jordynn and Layken. Dean had been an encouraging and supportive presence in my life since we became buddies in High School. He always reminded me of my potential and encouraged me to live up to it, which had fallen on deaf ears back in our high school days. We'd reconnected after we both divorced, and now he was back in my corner again, encouraging me to pursue my dreams.

Dean's family were like a second family to me. I cherished the time spent at his parent's apricot farm at Menindee on the beautiful Baaka, or Darling River. Menindee is on Barkindji country, about 100 km from Broken Hill. Deans' parents, Dick and Jan, were always a welcome dose of country hospitality. Their open arms and endless supply of love had been a nice respite from city life during post-divorce. I felt complete peace as we pulled into Dick and Jan's driveway. I was welcomed by their loving embrace, a cold beer and a star-filled sky.

After a restful night at the farm, we went to the caravan park to see Rach and Damo who were camping for the weekend. I made a very unwise decision to wipe myself out and forget about everything.

At some point in the night, someone brought out some hash cookies. Very drunk by now, I happily ate one thinking it would chill me out. The combination of weed and booze had the opposite effect. I vaguely recall wandering off, crying uncontrollably, releasing the trauma I had bottled up for so long.

Embarrassed by my emotional state, I walked down the dark, dusty dirt road out of the caravan park towards the main road and called the Broken Hill taxi number, looking for Uncle Dolly who by some miracle answered the phone. He was working the phones that night but, concerned about my well-being, sent a taxi on the 200 km round trip to collect me.

I meandered down the dirt road, paranoid about every sound I heard along the way. I could hear some Southern Boobook owls calling mo poke, mo poke. I saw the lights of a vehicle approaching and ran, jumping behind a tree to hide. I peered around the thick trunk, saw that the vehicle was a taxi, and ran out with my arms flailing around to flag it down. I must have looked like a wild animal. I jumped in the passenger seat in a state of paranoia, with a tear-stained face and wearing a beanie with two big pom poms on the top.

'I take it you're Belinda. Are you okay?'

'Yes, yes, let's go, let's go!'

The driver picked up the two-way radio and radioed back into base.

'You got a copy Dolly?'

'Go ahead.'

'I've got her,' he said. He replaced the receiver and drove off towards town.

As we pulled up, I looked at the meter. The fare was the cost of a plane ticket. I had no money on me. Seeing my panic, the driver reassured me. 'Dolly said you can fix him up later.' He delivered me to Bek's house and drove off.

I pulled my phone out of my pocket to see a heap of missed calls and voicemails from Dean. Shit, he would be wondering where the hell I had vanished to, in the middle of nowhere! I wasn't in any state to speak so I sent him a text letting him know I was back in Broken Hill.

'What the fuck!' was his response.

I'm sure he was wondering how the hell I got there but I couldn't deal with that then. I knocked quietly on Bek's front door and the sight of me almost gave her a heart attack. I apologised profusely as she made up a bed for me. The room was spinning and so was my head. I pulled the doona up to shut everything out.

I woke to a bustling house, kids running around, and Bek's best friend, Supa, sitting on the end of the lounge waiting for me to open my eyes. Supa has been in my life for as long as I can remember also. When Dylan was in hospital, she secretly transferred money into my bank account anonymously every single week to help me with expenses. Supa knew what it was like to be in my shoes. Her husband Alan had been in an accident years earlier and, thankfully, had recovered fully.

As memories of the night before began returning, I wished it was all just a bad dream.

Always the nurse, Bek was fussing, asking what on earth had happened.

'All I know is that I'm going to have a really big taxi fare to sort out with Uncle Dolly.'

'Geez Biz, you should have called me, I could have got a plane to come and get you cheaper than what that taxi fare will be.' Supa and Bek cracked up.

'*I'm no trouble at all,*' I said, shaking my head then cracking up laughing too.

Tambi picked me up later and I went to stay with her and her husband Rod for the night. Dean wasn't due back from the river until the following day and all my belongings were either at his house or his parents' farm, so I had to borrow some clothes from Rod to get me through the next two days. Tambi also saw the funny side to my adventures of the previous twenty-four hours and drew similarities to teenage Bizz.

'I don't think Dean is going to see a funny side to this,' I said.

'Probably not.'

'I hate to imagine what I looked like walking down that dusty road in the state I was in.'

Then, out of nowhere, creative inspiration struck.

'Tambi!! I need a pen quick!' She darted off and returned with a pen and paper.

I scribbled down the lyrics that had just popped into my head.

Ever since I could remember, writing poetry has come easily. In recent years I'd tried turning my love of poetry into writing song lyrics. Tambi insisted on hearing what I had written so I read them out loud for the first time.

Menindee Sky

At the end of this dirty and dusty road

There's a perfect Menindee Sky

My senses are pushed to overload.

As I think of my life gone by

The colours of this landscape

Are a picture-perfect sight.

Menindee you are a part of me.

And I know I'll be alright.

This is my land.

My outback home.

A part of me

No matter where I roam.

It's in my blood, it's in my veins.

From red dirt to sweeping plains

With stars that shine so bright above

It's in my blood it's in my veins.

From red dirt to sweeping plains

This is the land that I love.

My worries, they disappear

As I take a deep breath in

I close my eyelids tight.

And freedom spreads within

It's in my blood, it's in my veins.

From red dirt to sweeping plains

With stars that shine so bright above

It's in my blood it's in my veins.

From red dirt to sweeping plains

This is the land that I love.

'How the hell did you just pull that from your arse?' Tambi shook her head incredulously.

'Must have been the hash cookie.' We laughed so hard you'd have sworn we'd both just eaten one.

The next morning Dean messaged me. He was home, so I could come get my stuff. I entered the house hesitantly. Dean was unpacking his camping gear, and as he turned to greet me he gave my outfit a quick up and down, noticing I was wearing a man's clothes.

'Hi,' I said sheepishly.

'Hey.' He paused. 'Whose clothes are you wearing?'

'Rod's. I stayed at Tambi's last night.' He turned his back on me and continued unpacking.

'I'm really sorry, I feel terrible that I worried everyone.'

'How exactly did you get back to town, Bizz, did you hitchhike?'

'Of course not.' I paused. 'I did what you're supposed to do when you're intoxicated, I called a taxi,' I said indignantly.

'What the actual fuck. You called a taxi all the way to Menindee and back?'

'That's right, so really, I did the responsible thing.'

'Don't push it.' He shook his head. 'And exactly how much did that taxi cost?' I could see he was starting to soften...

'Well, Uncle Dolly managed to get the price down for me, family discount,' I said proudly.

'How much Bizz?' he pushed.

'Two hundred and fifty dollars, but that was down from four hundred,' I smiled. 'I really am sorry mofo,' – my term of endearment for Dean – 'that will be the last time I eat a hash cookie, I swear! Do you want me to stay somewhere else until I go home?'

'Of course not.' I gave him a hug. He never could stay angry with me.

'Are you okay?' His anger was making way for concern. I said I was fine, but I knew it would be a while before I was.

Dean and I have always had a special connection. He'd taken me on numerous camping trips in the years following my divorce and taught me how to fish. I'll never forget my first catch, standing on a giant log on the riverbank as I wound the line in, full of excitement. I'd hooked a decent-sized cod. As the fish got closer, the movement on the line (coupled with a beer or two) made me lose my footing and land on the wet river sand below, much to the amusement of my experienced fishing instructor. Dean later joked that I wasn't the only one who secured a good catch that day, when our friendship crossed the boundaries, and we became lovers.

That was in the early days of post-divorce for us both. We were two souls connected but trying to heal individual hurts. It was never going to work long-term. They say people come into your life for a season, a reason, or a lifetime. My friendship with Dean will be all three. We were lovers for a season, reconnected for a reason, and our relationship, rooted in a deep friendship, will be for a lifetime.

Some say you can never go back after crossing those boundaries. A 'friends with benefits' deal with one of your oldest and dearest friends was quite reckless with hindsight, but I'm glad we managed to maintain our friendship.

I headed back to Brisbane with a new song inside me. It felt great to have my creative juices flowing again. I knew just who to take it to: my old mate Buzz Talay. Buzz and his wife Shelley's son Ned is the same age as Hudson. The boys played AFL together throughout primary school and we often socialised on weekend camping trips and motorbike riding. Buzz had even helped the boys form their own primary school band which they decided to call The Red Hot Chicken Feathers. Band practice was held weekly at Ned's house with Hudson as drummer. Shelley and I job-shared for a while, at a seismic exploration company. Buzz worked there in logistics. We were at the company's workshop in west Brisbane, cleaning cars when the crews came back from a hitch. Shelley and I both moved on to job share at Merthyr Law, where I was still working. Shelley had left for another job, but we remained close friends, and she was a significant presence in my life after Dylan's accident, making many home cooked meals for us and helping however she could.

Buzz, from country NSW, is a singer and songwriter and a veteran of the country music scene. For twenty-five years he's been playing music in Australia as well as the US and New Zealand. He is a regular at Tamworth Country Music Festival, Mud Bulls & Music and The Urban Country Music Festival.

I was still working on my screenplay and, since Menindee was one of the locations in the story, I thought 'Menindee Sky' could be a perfect song for the soundtrack. I approached Buzz with my lyrics and asked if he would be interested in collaborating.

Buzz roped in his fellow band members Desi J Johnson, the tattooed drummer and coolest cat you could ever meet, his lifelong best buddy Pedlar Staines on guitar, and Tony Black on bass. In no time at all we had composed an epic tune.

After several private rehearsals, Buzz finally invited me over one evening after work to listen to the band perform 'Menindee Sky'. I arrived at Buzz's home studio, filled with anticipation and excitement.

The little studio space instantly makes you feel like you're part of something magical. I took in the walls displaying music memorabilia, posters, and photos. As the band began to play, I felt goosebumps all over my body. 'Menindee Sky' took me on a musical journey that I could hear and feel. I can't describe how it felt to hear my words put to music. My whole life I had expressed my thoughts and feelings in poetry, so it was a powerful moment. Buzz still had one more ace up his sleeve, securing Golden Guitar–winning fiddle player Pixie Jenkins to play on the track.

Dean and I at the prom

CHAPTER EIGHT

I Bought a Bus

It was 2013 and our little family had some big changes ahead. Miki had graduated from high school and had been offered a spot in the young conservatorium choir as well as a place at Queensland University of Technology (QUT) to study creative arts. She had also joined my mum and I working at Merthyr Law, so we were three generations of women working in the same office.

Merthyr was a great place to work. Our bosses, Steve and Kieran, often organised team building days which included clay pigeon shooting, murder mystery evenings and barefoot bowls. What I loved and admired them for most was the flexibility they allowed their casual employees, supporting job share for those with outside study or family commitments. If you were willing to work hard, they supported their employees in return.

I had a core group of workmates that had become like a second family post-divorce. The bonds cemented even more after Dylan's accident. I'd often spend Friday nights after work unwinding over a drink or two with the team: Marie, Kim, Shannon, Courtney, Jacqui, Natalie, Lauren, mum, and Miki now that she had turned eighteen.

Hudson had relocated to a high school close to home to begin his grade nine studies. The long travel to school the previous year on top of everything else had been too much for him so I had enrolled him at Holland Park High where Miki had completed her final two years of high school. It was a small school but had a really nurturing environment and a great bunch of kids. Hudson quickly made new friends, including his best buddy to this day, Hayden. Those two have been through more together than any kids should have to. We love Hayden like one of our own and Hudson is a valued member of his family.

Dylan was home all day, sleeping or playing Xbox. He had begun working on a giant Iron Man display with the same devotion and focus Tony Stark had put into building his suit.

I decided a real-world project might be beneficial for his mental and physical well-being. I urged him to start looking for a cheap car that he could work on, getting him outside in the fresh air and, hopefully, assisting with his rehabilitation. He had always been good with his hands and mechanically minded. This passion might help him move forward.

Dylan's friends Robbie and Ellen were looking for a new car. Dylan went along with them to numerous car yards. They returned a few hours later and Dylan, emotionally distraught, went straight to his room.

'What happened?' I asked.

'A salesman at the last car yard referred to Dylan as a retard, and implied he didn't require any service for that reason,' Ellen explained.

What the actual fuck! 'What exactly happened?'

Ellen explained the salesman had called Dylan a retard and that she and Robbie defended their friend.

I thanked Robbie and Ellen for calling the guy out. We arranged to go back to the car yard together the following afternoon to request an apology.

I walked Robbie and Ellen to the front door, then went to check on Dylan, knocking gently on his bedroom door before entering.

'Am I retarded? I know I'm different now, but do I come across as being simple?' he asked with great sadness.

'Please do not let an uneducated man's words inside your head. You're a walking miracle. You've overcome insurmountable obstacles and fought your way back from near death. That takes incredible power of the mind. Iron Man may be your superhero, but you are mine.'

I was trying to sound calm, but inside my blood was boiling.

The next afternoon I met Robbie and Ellen at the car yard after work. They pointed out the salesman before we went inside. I asked to speak to the dealership manager. We explained what had happened the night before and he sat, unmoved, behind his desk, unwilling to consider the issue about his employee. In fact, he informed us, he was aware of the incident and said, 'I don't know what you want me to do, I can't control what people say!'

The lack of care shown by management compounded the injustice. I said we wanted him and his staff to understand the impact that discriminatory words and behaviour can have. I said Dylan deserved the same service offered to other customers looking to buy a car. I left the dealership angrier than when I had arrived.

I was exhausted and overwhelmed and I wondered if I had enough energy for another battle. But I couldn't just let this go. I contacted the head office of the car yard chain and received no response. I went higher up the ladder to the company that owned the chain and again got no response.

By now there was no letting go. The feelings of injustice grew every time the company failed to deal with a serious complaint. I approached the anti-discrimination commission to lodge a formal complaint against the individual and the company who employed him. The Anti-Discrimination Commission Queensland, or ADCQ, accepted our case. A date was set for a mediation session with a representative from the car yard and me at the ADCQ Brisbane office. They would ignore us no longer.

If you are neutral in situations of injustice, you have chosen the side of the oppressor, said Archbishop Desmond Tutu.

The time had come for us to sell our family home. I needed to refinance the house and take out a new mortgage so that Paul's name was no longer on the loan. I had approached the bank to discuss options for refinancing but being single with inconsistent income meant this was not an option.

This had been our family home for sixteen years. Almost every memory of my children's childhood was made in that house. It was a beautiful two-storey house with a swimming pool, lock up garage and granny flat downstairs where my mother lived. It was always a bustling and warm home, filled with the sound of children's laughter, not just my own kids, but also of their friends, many of whom were like part of our family.

We were especially close to our neighbours Maryanne and Don who were like an aunty and uncle to our kids. Maryanne and I would often go for a walk and discuss life, travel, and our dreams.

Michelle, Ron and the kids lived across the road. We had been friends going on fifteen years, but had become especially close since my divorce, and even more so since Dylan's accident. They were the kind of friends you didn't need an invitation from, you just turned up on the doorstep and let yourself in. Ronny had earned the nickname of Mr. Roofus due to the many evenings we would spend sitting on their roof, beer in hand, looking up at stars. The kids often joined us, including Candy and Jase, their two older kids who had moved out of home and had families of their own. Something about Ronny reminded me of my grandfather George whom I had adored. Both kind and gentle souls with a great sense of humour.

The support Michelle, Ron and their whole family had given was immeasurable. It felt like the end of an era. We weren't just leaving a home, we were leaving a community.

The concern that was weighing most heavily on me at the time was our finances. We had bought the house when the housing market was a lot more affordable, so the mortgage repayments were substantially less than the rental market. It would mean doubling my weekly budget to put a roof over our heads.

Unable to switch off my mind, I was having difficulty sleeping. I would often lie awake for hours staring at the ceiling searching for answers to what seemed like a never-ending list of questions. One night as I crawled into bed, I mentally asked the universe to just give me one sign that everything was going to be okay. I awoke the following morning from the weirdest dream that felt more like a vision. I had dreamt about a big blue bus that reminded me of the magic school bus. I felt a sense of urgency to find it.

I tried to push the idea out of my mind and go about my day, but I couldn't get the vision of this bus from my mind. I decided, later, to put a post up on Facebook asking if anyone knew of any buses for sale. An hour or so later I received a message from my friend Caroline who sent me a link to a bus she had found for sale at a bus yard at Archerfield in Brisbane's west.

Holy shit balls of fire! It looked exactly like the one in my dream. I couldn't believe it. Crazy as it seemed, I knew I had to buy that bus. I didn't know how I was going to buy the bus, but I knew that I had to for two key reasons: so I could use it to raise awareness for people affected by brain injury, and so I would have a place to live if I could not afford a house down the track. My only obstacle was I wouldn't have the funds until I sold the house and there was no way of knowing how long that would take.

A few days later Kerry called to check in and see how Dylan was doing. I told her of our plan to buy him a car to work on until he could drive again. She thought this was a great idea and said it would be a form of rehabilitation to do some of the hands-on kind of work he had been doing before his accident.

'I thought you were going to say you were buying him a bus after seeing your Facebook post the other day,' she laughed.

'Actually, I dreamt that I am meant to use it to raise awareness for brain injury survivors.'

I filled her in on the incident at the car yard, our case with the anti-discrimination commission, and how it was the catalyst for my growing determination to be a moving billboard for brain injury awareness.

'Bizz, that is an amazing idea, I can lend you the money until you sell the house.'

It was an extremely generous offer, but I said there was no way I could possibly accept. Kerry would not take no for an answer, arguing it was a brilliant idea and, speaking as a physiotherapist who specialised in the brain, the awareness was much needed.

I truly believe we come across earth angels on our journey whose light shines brightly when we are surrounded in darkness. Kerry was without a doubt a guardian, guiding me through the most challenging of times.

Two weeks later I was the proud owner of an ex-Brisbane City Council Mercedes Benz bus, and she was a blue beauty. She had low kilometres because she had come from Stradbroke Island, but had a bit of wear and tear, and some body rust.

The problem was I couldn't drive it. It required a medium rigid truck licence. I figured that was a minor detail I could figure out later. The more pressing issue was where to park it! There was no room at the house, and it was about to go on the market. Then a kind offer came from Paul to park it at the landfill where he was the foreman. The premises were gated and locked at night and protected by security, so I graciously accepted the little step forward in thawing the ice between us.

The day finally arrived for our mediation with the car yard at ADCQ. I felt nervous but mostly determined. I arrived at their Brisbane offices accompanied by my ever-supportive and present mum, Frannie. Dylan had chosen not to attend personally, but fully supported what we were doing on his behalf.

After a short wait, an ADCQ representative came to speak with us, explaining how the mediation process would unfold. We were led into the meeting room and seated on the opposite side of the table to the employee who had discriminated against Dylan and a representative from the company.

They were given the opportunity to speak first, finally apologising. The employee said he didn't mean to cause any harm to Dylan, that he could now see how his words and actions may have done so. He offered to make amends by coming to mow our lawn or help us in some other way. The company representative informed us that he had only recently been made aware of the situation, which to me highlighted gross negligence within the company.

When it was my time to speak, I accepted his apology but then turned my attention to the company representative and proceeded to tell him that I had tried to deal with this issue through every level of their management but to no avail. I expressed my disappointment that at no stage of the process did anyone inquire about Dylan's well-being and explained to them both the months of intense medical treatment Dylan had just endured after a near fatal car accident. The discriminatory treatment he received at their business had damaged his confidence and self-esteem. Every person has a right to service and to be treated with respect.

The mediation concluded, we went home to discuss with Dylan what action we thought would be fair and reasonable. Despite our precarious financial position, we did not want money, but I felt it was important they do something to help Dylan move forward, since their actions, or rather inaction, had set him back. We also wanted them to implement anti-discrimination training for all employees and make changes within their company structure to better deal with complaints in the future.

This was about education and responsibility. After careful consideration we sent them a letter outlining our wishes. Dylan was about to undergo specialised driver training with an occupational therapist which was very expensive, so we thought a request for them to fund that would be a fair contribution to his personal rehabilitation and recovery. We also suggested a donation be made to Sporting Wheelies, and training be undertaken specifically for the car salesman who discriminated against Dylan so he would understand that his behaviour has no place in our society.

With the assistance of Kimmie, one of my lawyer colleagues, we drafted a letter outlining our wishes 'without prejudice' as well as a reminder of Parliament's Anti-Discrimination Act.

A week later we were notified they had agreed to everything we had requested.

1. An apology.

2. Payment made for Dylan's driver training with an occupational therapist to help him move forward in his recovery.

3. Confirmation that all current employees within the company would undergo training in relation to effectively dealing with complaints in the future.

4. The individual who discriminated against Dylan undergo individual training.

5. A donation of $1000 be made to the Sporting Wheelies.

We declined the offer of services from the yard and signed off on the agreement feeling exhausted. It was hard to feel like there was any victory in this moment because nothing would undo the damage done to Dylan and the amount of precious time and energy wasted on the case when there were far more important things to be focusing on.

CHAPTER NINE

Menindee Sky

In August 2013 my magic bus set off on its maiden voyage. On board was my then business partner Paige, Buzz, Pedlar and a small film crew.

I had managed to secure emerging director Ryan Unicomb to direct our music video along with his colleague Jordan as our assistant director. We were joined by one of my favourite humans, a talented young videographer named Jacques Ollivier. I'd had the pleasure of working with all three of these young men on some short films when I was doing makeup. They were excited to join our *Priscilla Queen of the Desert*-inspired journey to Broken Hill. The plan was to film a music video for 'Menindee Sky' and, at the same time, scout locations for my screenplay 'Chasing Jon'.

Buzz roped in Hungarian dancer Bolage (Bolly for short) to drive the bus, since I still couldn't drive it. Bolly was happy to jump on board just for the adventure.

I had planned the trip to coincide with Brain Injury Awareness Week, an opportunity to raise awareness and funds for Synapse – Australia's Brain Injury Organisation – by selling beanies, part of their Bang on a Beanie campaign. The campaign was to encourage discussion around brain injury and the invisible barriers people living with it deal with every day.

The bus was loaded with boxes of blue beanies, film equipment, and musical instruments. We finally hit the road in August after only a few short months of planning. The slogans 'Bang on a Beanie' and 'Chasing Jon' were emblazoned in bright colours on the exterior of the bus. My good luck charm, a plastic Jon Bon Jovi doll, was stuck on the dashboard. I was reminded of one of my favourite Bon Jovi songs 'Lost Highway' as we drove off into the sunrise. I joked with the crew that the doll was my plastic dashboard Jesus watching over us. Everyone needs a mascot, right?

Five hours into our trip we did a tyre in the township of Moree. With such a tight schedule we had no time to lose. We pulled into the local tyre shop where we were met with some delightful country hospitality. After asking what 'Bang on a Beanie' meant came an offer to fix the tyre immediately for free. We thanked the team at the tyre shop profusely and gifted them some beanies, then hit the road towards Coonabarabran, our overnight destination.

Ryan is a Coona boy and was excited to have the opportunity to spend some time with his family, so after a quick meeting with a reporter from the local paper, Ryan and Jordan said goodnight for the evening.

The rest of us went the Golden Sea Dragon Chinese Restaurant, highly recommended by Ryan. The restaurant is a hidden gem with the authentic Chinese decor and delicious menu.

Over dinner Bolly said he was concerned about something mechanical and wanted to check the bus over. We were all tired, so after dinner headed to the John Oxley Caravan Park to check in to our cabins.

Bolly, Buzz and Pedlar went to work on the bus, quickly locating the problem, a minor issue with the power steering belt. A few quick adjustments were made, and the issue rectified. We all went to bed exhausted after our first big day on the Bang on a Beanie Bus.

We all struggled to drag our butts out of bed in near-zero temperatures the next morning. It was a big change from the Queensland winters we were all acclimatised to.

We met Ryan and Jordan at the Coonabarabran Bakery, grabbed some much-needed coffee and breakfast, and hit the road.

A few hours down the track, in the town of Warren, the gearstick detached from the gearbox as we rounded a corner. A bush on the gearstick had collapsed. Bolly managed to use what little momentum the bus still had to roll around the corner, stopping on a side street. This was no small matter, and nothing like the previous mishaps. This time we were well and truly fucked!

There was no way known to man, woman or dog that we were going to find a bus part for a Mercedes Benz bus in this rural township with a population of approximately 2,500 people. Not in a hurry. Our very tight schedule was thrown out the window. I could feel the panic rising in me at the prospect of being stranded indefinitely.

Bolly and Buzz examined the gearshift. I stepped outside for some much-needed cool air on my face. It was a welcome relief as I paced around the bus pleading with the universe for assistance.

As I circled the bus, I saw Buzz descend the stairs, his attention focused on an object in the grass. He knelt and picked it up to get a closer look. I took a photo of him at that moment, which I'm glad of, because what happened next was unbelievable.

'It's a plastic piece from a bottle top and it looks like the exact shape and size of the part we need,' Buzz said.

He climbed back onto the bus and handed the bit of plastic to Bolly, who turned it around slowly in his hands inspecting every millimetre.

'You're right, this actually might work.'

Buzz and Bolly went to work molding the plastic with a piece of metal until it was the perfect fit. With the gearstick back in place, Bolly roared the bus back to life and gave the gearstick a thrust. You could have knocked us down with a feather – the darn thing actually worked!

Paige and I screamed with excitement. My young film friends sat speechless at the back of the bus. You really couldn't make this shit up, I thought, as we resumed our journey.

'I always said it was a magic bus.'

I think Buzz had his own magic going on too.

When we finally made it into Broken Hill it was dark. It was the first time most of the crew had been to the Hill, so they were all excited. We were also, appropriately, staying at the iconic Palace Hotel. If you're going to do a *Priscilla*-inspired Road trip, the Palace is non-negotiable.

We entered the foyer in awe of the murals that cover the walls. Every step up the staircase to the first-floor budget rooms we had booked was a feast for the eyes. The men were sharing dorm-style rooms, and Paige and I had a small room with two single beds, a bar fridge and kettle. There would be no 'Priscilla Suite' for us on this trip, but Paige and I felt like two schoolgirls on an adventure as we washed up and climbed into bed that first night, talking and laughing.

We rose early and wandered down to Subway in the main street for breakfast and a morning meeting with Dean who filled us in on the progress for our Menindee locations. He and his parents, Dick and Jan, worked hard, securing every one of them. Dick had worked especially tirelessly in the lead-up to our trip, first by visiting people in the township to play them the song, which he himself had fallen in love with. Then by organising locations and our campsite at a station for the music video shoot.

Our day one agenda was a visit to ABC radio for an interview about 'Menindee Sky' and the Bang on a Beanie campaign. I was extremely nervous as we entered the ABC Radio building. This would be my first-ever radio interview, so I was grateful Buzz was with me.

Seated in the radio booth, ABC veteran and host of Outback Outlook Chris Jeremy, instantly put me at ease with his opening question.

'What is a former local Broken Hill person doing back in Broken Hill with a big blue bus wearing a big blue beanie?'

It felt like talking to an old friend. We discussed the purpose behind the Bang on a Beanie campaign, my personal journey with Dylan, and the connection between music and healing that led to the writing of 'Menindee Sky'. Buzz then took the lead, talking about how the song was a well-deserved musical ode to the township of Menindee on the Darling River, and how my love for the town and its people had brought a wealth of creative inspiration. As a thank you, the town and its surroundings, and some of the locals, would feature in the music video.

Chris wrapped up the interview, and afterwards Buzz told me how proud he was of me for speaking from the heart with such clarity. I felt a little taller as we left the building and boarded the bus for Silverton to scout locations for

'Chasing Jon'. The 25 km drive from Broken Hill to Silverton is famous for its thirty-nine dips on a winding outback road, especially bouncy on our short bus ride to the outback village. We turned off the bitumen on to the famous red dirt road, excited to see donkeys out front of the Silverton pub. Silverton has been the setting for numerous films, television series and commercials over the years. On the walls are photographs from these, along with art made from beer cans. Joke cards spotlighting the Aussie sense of humour hang from the ceiling. The country-themed beer garden and a stage made from an old truck was a hit with Buzz and Pedlar. The beer garden hosts country music singers who perform for the tourists and Broken Hillians. The Silverton Hotel is known as one of the best outback pubs.

Up the hill from the pub is a location everyone on the bus was keen to visit: the Mad Max Museum. It would be my first visit to the museum, only established in 2010. We parked up at the museum entrance just as the founder and owner, Adrian Bennett, stepped out the front door. Adrian greeted us enthusiastically as, one by one, we entered the museum. He wanted to know what 'Bang on a Beanie' was about.

I explained the campaign, and he asked if I knew someone with a brain injury.

'My son has a brain injury.'

'I have a son with a brain injury too!'

We shared our sons' stories and, instantly, this total stranger became a lifelong friend. We shared a hug, and the unspoken parental pain we knew each other had experienced.

We were given a personal tour by Adrian and his wife Linda, who refused to let any of us pay the entrance fee. Adrian even did a short chat to camera for us, describing how he had transformed his passion for Dr George Miller's post-apocalyptic *Mad Max* film franchise into a museum in the outback. Memorabilia, props, costumes, photos and even vehicles from the films fill the small space along with the warmth, heart and hospitality of the owners.

We returned to the Palace Hotel via a pitstop at Reganovich's for some hot chips with chicken salt for dinner.

Paige and I settled in for the night. Paige's generosity of spirit and support for me and my dreams had known no bounds. This gift of time was helping me to get to know a little more about her hopes and dreams also.

On day two our first location was the Broken Hill Film Studios. The council had recently purchased the old power station as a new studio space to boost filmmaking in the region and in preparation for the new *Mad Max* film, *Fury Road*. The film had been scheduled to film there in 2011 but heavy rains had turned the desert landscape into lush green meadows. After several delays, the production went elsewhere.

We were given a private tour of the studios by Screen Broken Hill representative Lyndall Roberts. The space was impressive, and we were more than a little excited to discover the Priscilla Bus covered with a big tarp. We gently rolled back the tarp and stepped inside to a disco sea of glitter. The flamboyant décor made my bus look as bland as a piece of toast.

Being in such an impressive space and seeing all the film memorabilia we had over the past few days filled me with inspiration. I was more determined than ever to bring my own dream project to life.

A two-minute drive away, in South Broken Hill, is Bells Milk Bar. Bells was one of my favourite hangouts as a teenager and another iconic location I had written into my screenplay. The milk bar is still decked out in its original 1950s decor with a museum and gift shop. Bells are famous for making their own syrups that are sold around the country. Their soda spiders were a huge hit with the crew.

The crew wandered around the milk bar, taking in the 1950s vibes while I introduced myself to the owner, Jason King. Jason was from the same area of Brisbane we called home, but he had fallen in love with Bells and Broken Hill and had relocated in 2004.

Jason shared my passion for filmmaking and was a keen videographer at the time. He kindly offered to assist in any way. At the time I couldn't know what a key part in my career and life Jason would play, and that this was the beginning of a new friendship.

As we drove back into town, our interview came over the radio. Bolly pulled the bus over, and we huddled around close and listened. It's hard to listen to yourself speak! I felt so awkward, but Paige reached out and gave me a reassuring squeeze and the boys all nodded their encouragement. Before we knew it, Buzz was wrapping up the interview by introducing 'Menindee Sky'. Hearing it play on the radio for the very first time was an unbelievable moment for me. To hear words you've written from the heart, about the land I felt so connected to, was indescribable. I looked around at the faces of the amazing humans, all there in one way or another because of that song. Music really is the greatest connector. That moment will always be one of the highlights of my life.

We were up before dawn the next day to get on the road to Menindee for our music video shoot. We were filming in multiple locations over two days, but our first destination was Dick and Jan's apricot farm.

The premise of the story for the music video was two people's lifelong relationship with each other and the land they loved so much. Jordy and Layken were playing the younger versions of the characters when they first became friends as school kids, Dean and I the middle-aged version, and Dick and Jan the older version of the characters.

After introducing Dick and Jan to the crew, Ryan, Jordan and Jacques jumped on the quads to explore the property. One of my favourite shots from the video is a shot straight down the centre of a row of apricot trees. When drought came a few years later, Dick and Jan would lose those crops, so to have this on film is like a time capsule for them, capturing such an important part of their life.

In filmmaking, scenes are never shot in sequential order, so we shot the final scene next, of three versions of the characters sitting on the same wooden seat on the property. Ryan had a great ability as a director, and with this one sequence he captured the essence of the story, and that the characters were being shown through the passage of time.

We wrapped at the farm by midday and headed to our next location, Bootingee Station, owned by Dick and Jan's friends Stuey and Michelle Oates. The station was on the banks of the river, so we were able to get all our station and river footage here, including some ripper shots of Buzz inside the shearing shed. The sheep were well behaved extras. In fact, all our extras did a fantastic job, considering they had never been in front of the camera before.

We shot the kids flying a kite, Dean and I yabbying, and of course it wouldn't be the outback without a shot of an old Toyota Landcruiser. Those vehicles are synonymous with Australian outback life. They go and go, which is why they hold their value so well.

As the sun began to set, we drove up to Maidens Hotel where Buzz and Pedlar performed a free acoustic gig, launching 'Menindee Sky' to the locals who featured in the music video.

Ryan wanted to get a shot of Dean and I walking into the packed pub and taking a seat at the bar. We had to reshoot this numerous times because Dean kept looking at the camera which made me laugh. On another take an extremely intoxicated man started asking questions, like was I a rockstar or something, all dressed up. We managed to pull ourselves together long enough to get the shot, although if you watch closely, you can see Dean look up and around the camera during that scene in an attempt not to look at the camera.

I could finally relax after the shoot and soak the moment in. Dick and Jan stood beside me arm in arm at the bar while Buzz performed 'Menindee Sky'. With tears in his eyes, Dick hugged me tight and told me how proud he was of me, and Jan said how surreal the experience was for them. Family is not always about blood, but those who are there for us no matter what. The Arnolds are the family I got to choose, and they will always be my Menindee Sky.

We wrapped at Maidens and drove back to our campsite to get some campfire shots, then crawled into our swags exhausted. I was spent, but still in awe of the stars that shone so brightly without the glare of city lights. When you stop being busy for a moment and just sit in nature, you remember that everything is connected. In the absolute wonder of nature you can see, hear and feel everything! For me, the land is sacred.

Only a few years later the beautiful Barka would run dry. Dick Arnold went viral holding up some of the dead fish in the now famous fish kill video. The river and water really are our lifeblood. There are many things we can live without, but water is not one of them.

We said our goodbyes to the Arnolds and Oates families, thanking them profusely for all they had done to help bring this music video to life.

The music video went on to be broadcast on Foxtel's CMC (Country Music Channel), an unreal experience for my first-ever time producing. It was only possible because the entire team contributed to something special.

Bolly, Me, Ryan, Paige, Jordan and Pedlar on our road trip to Broken Hill raising awareness for Bang on a Beanie

Paige and I at The Palace Hotel
Photo credit: Jacques Ollivier

Buzz and Bolly doing bush repairs to the bus

Jacques, Jordon and Ryan on the big red seat in Broken Hill

CHAPTER TEN
End of an Era

I settled back into my familiar life. Though all that was familiar would soon be gone with the sale of our family home. The thought of sifting through twenty years of memories overwhelmed me. A floodgate of memories opened as I sorted through boxes upon boxes of works of art, hand-made by my kids, including pasta necklaces, Mother's Day cards and school projects. Each discovery brought a wave of emotion, from joy to grief. I remembered the little hands that had crafted these treasures, and how I missed those little people who had been the centre of my world. Becoming a mum at the age of eighteen means missing years of personal growth that travel and education bring for many young adults. A controlling relationship in my teenage years also impacted my confidence, but I loved being a stay-at-home mum. I was determined my kids would have the opportunity to discover who they were, and I encouraged their individuality.

My days as a young mother were filled with volunteer activities at their school, assisting with daily reading, math's activities, tuck-shop. I especially enjoyed accompanying classes on school excursions. Afternoons were usually spent driving my kids around.

Dylan played baseball, like his dad, took guitar lessons and studied karate. He also liked tinkering in the shed, inventing things, and tending to the wounded animals that he was forever bringing home to save. He and his two best friends, Chris and Nathanial, were inseparable. I remember them making a pact to someday open a café together and call it the ChrisDilNat Café.

I will never forget the first time I took the boys in to see Dylan after he was woken from his coma. The first thing he said was 'ChrisDilNat'. We all cried amongst the confusion, his memories were still there, albeit slightly jumbled.

School was not the easiest time for Dylan, he had auditory processing difficulties and was at times bullied. He was lucky to have received extra assistance from Tanya, a teacher aid, throughout primary school. Tanya was kind and patient and would become a friend to us all. She made Dylan feel seen and heard and knew that not all students learn the same way. Never was this more apparent than the day Dylan came home with a poem she had given him called 'Johnny's got a pocket full of dreams', about a boy who carries the small treasures he has collected in his pocket along with his dreams, before the world becomes tough. I thought about the poem and that small boy with dreams, whose heart I wanted to protect. How tough the road had been already for him, as well as Mikaela, and Hudson, losing their innocence so young.

Mikaela was our little social butterfly. As a child she wanted to do, try and experience everything! Her afternoons were filled with dance classes, singing lessons, guitar and soccer practice. At school she was involved in various groups and ensembles from choir to playing the violin in the string orchestra, on top of her extremely busy social calendar.

I often worried she was doing too much, but I didn't want to stand in the way so supported her dedication. I have many fond memories of styling Miki's hair in preparation for the many eisteddfods she competed in. The gift of one-on-one time with my girl was that she would enthusiastically share her hopes and dreams, as well as her disappointments.

One year she talked me into volunteering to do makeup and paint sets for the school play, which would eventually lead to me pursuing my own career in the arts. My fearless little girl took on all challenges with a grit and determination I had never known, and, in some ways, she had become my teacher.

Miki was and is extremely close to both her brothers. Being almost five years older than Hudson, she was like a second mum.

He was an extremely active kid, and as a toddler we needed multiple pairs of eyes on him because he was always off exploring something, a million miles an hour, which often resulted in some form of injury.

His life had begun with near death, for us both. I had an undiagnosed case of placenta praevia which made me extremely ill in the latter stages of my pregnancy. I knew something was wrong so insisted on being induced days before my due date. My intuition was confirmed when I haemorrhaged. If we hadn't been at the hospital, I would have bled out and both Hudson and I may have died before an ambulance could have made it to us.

It was an extremely traumatic birth for us both, and we both missed that skin-to-skin bonding because I was given multiple blood transfusions whilst recovering from an emergency caesarean. The first photo taken of Hudson in the hospital shows the face of an old soul, his hands clenched together in little fists. My little fighter was fearless.

Being the youngest child, he was brought straight into the frenetic pace of running around after two older siblings who adored him. Hudson's interests were like mine as a kid. He took drumming lessons and was passionate about sports, mostly AFL and basketball. I joined his AFL team as team manager for a period and will never forget his pride the year his team played halftime at a Brisbane Lions game. He ran off the field to the stands where we were seated.

'This is the proudest moment of my life,' he said.

It was one of my proudest moments too, watching him, so young, smashing goals.

Hudson's big brother Dylan was his adventure buddy and best friend.

I gifted myself the time to pore over every page of my extensive photo album collection, reliving each and every moment captured on film and in my heart.

As I turned the page, a familiar cheeky face smiled back at me. My dear friend Ronny, a true Aussie larrikin and legend who had been a presence in my life the preceding years. He had been battling cancer all year and had recently received the devastating news that it was terminal. He only had weeks to live. My heart broke for Michelle and the kids, and for me also.

In true Ronny style, he had decided he wanted to have a Father's Day BBQ with family and friends in the park so he could spend time with his favourite people. He was very gracious, making sure those who loved him had the opportunity to express what they needed to. It was obvious he was suffering, but he never complained, even though he had every right to.

The BBQ was on the first day of spring, the sun's warmth on us as we arrived at the park to be greeted by Ronny wearing his usual concreter's thongs and a bright Hawaiian shirt. Physically he was a shadow of his former self, but his spirit was as colourful as the flowers blooming with the arrival of spring.

I felt honoured to be included in this celebration of an amazing father, husband, and friend. A man who had a gift for helping us heal when we were hurting. I think he struggled with knowing that he couldn't do that for us now.

A few short weeks later he would leave us. For me, it felt like the worst possible time to move away from Shell and the kids as they grieved the loss of this incredible man. But we couldn't delay the sale any longer. The house sold in the first week, so the kids and I moved into a rental in Holland Park near Hudson's school to begin the next chapter of our lives.

There was an exciting new opportunity for me. One day, out of the blue, I got a message from a friend of Paige's that I had met in Sydney the previous year. Her name was Mikki too, but with two K's.

Mikki worked in the film and music industries and was soon coming to Brisbane to work on Pink's Australian tour. She wanted to know if I would be interested in working as a Live Nation VIP party host at the Brisbane concerts on the tour. I couldn't believe my luck.

I was excited to finally meet Kat, who Mikki had accurately described as a little lady with a big personality, and the rest of the VIP assistants. I hit it off instantly with Dyna, who had just moved to Brisbane with her husband John and young family from Grafton. DJ Mark and I also hit it off, with our shared passion for music and the arts.

We would begin our shift by packing the VIP gift bags, before checking in people who had purchased VIP packages.

This was a whole new working experience for me. I had never worked in customer service before, and I loved the buzz of meeting people who were about to see their favourite music icons perform.

After check-in we would work in the VIP party room, spray-painting glitter tattoos on people. At the end of our shift, Mr Love, the head of catering at the Brisbane Entertainment Centre, would escort us to catering for dinner.

It was beyond cool to be in the buzz of the backstage area with crew, roadies and band members.

I loved walking those backstage hallways, the excitement of a concert building around me. The best part was after dinner when we got to watch the concert up front.

It was the kind of experience a Broken Hill kid could only ever dream about. I hadn't even been to a real concert until I was nineteen, when I attended my first ever Bon Jovi concert in Adelaide with Paul and one of my high school buddies, Andreana.

I worked on all eight of Pink's Brisbane shows and became a regular VIP worker for Live Nation with Kat, Dyna, John and Mark. I had found a whole new circle of friends in this music world. My favourite thing was meet and greets, seeing people meet their music idols. It would often move me to tears because I understood the feeling of loving a band so much and feeling a deep personal connection to their music. I wondered if I would ever get the opportunity to meet the man and the band whose lyrics I had connected with for most of my life, Bon Jovi.

I was still pouring everything I had into my screenplay, which was ever evolving.

Bon Jovi were heading back to Australia for their Because We Can tour, and I was determined to try and get the media to pick up a story about a local fan who was writing a feature film inspired by their music. The band have a very large and loyal Australian fan base that have stuck with them over the vast span of their musical career. We often refer to ourselves as the Jovi Nation. Others may not get it because 'it's a Jovi thing'. I was hoping this could be my chance to get on Jon's radar and tell him how much his music had influenced my life!

I enlisted the services of a media and marketing company to send out a media release and see if anyone was interested in my fan story.

Dylan was also beginning a new chapter. After months of driver training with an occupational therapist, he was given his driver's licence back and could return to doing some landscaping. It was a huge step forward for him, giving him back some much-needed independence.

There were still lingering fears holding Dylan back. He was nervous about flying, post-accident, worried there would be pressure in his brain at a high altitude. To help him move past this, I had encouraged him to do a short flight with me to Sydney, to the wax museum to see the Iron Man display. With Bon Jovi touring at that time, we decided to attend their Because We Can tour while we were there. I had always promised to take Dylan to a Bon Jovi concert someday.

Dylan was extremely anxious as we boarded our flight to Sydney. I had packed ear plugs in case the noise became overwhelming for him. It did, and so did the confined space, but he managed to get through the one-hour flight. We were soon in a taxi to our accommodation in Darling Harbour where Madame Tussauds wax museum is located.

Dylan adopted his best Tony Stark near the life size Iron Man wax figure, proudly posing so I could snap his photo. We were like big kids as we enacted scenes from some of our favourite films at each display, from *ET* to Alfred Hitchcock's *Psycho*. It felt so good to have a carefree moment with Dylan after a harrowing year and a half.

Later that evening, as we travelled by train to Sydney's ANZ Stadium, I sensed Dylan's fatigue. As we took our seats on the stadium floor, I was concerned I had made a mistake scheduling so much for one day. I was still trying to navigate Dylan's needs post-injury. He insisted he was okay, but I sensed he didn't want to let me down, so I suggested we leave early to avoid the crowds. We had shared such an incredible day together, seeing the things that inspired us, so it didn't matter that we didn't see the whole show. I may have had some Jovi Girl guilt as we walked out mid–Bon Jovi concert, but considering I was attending the Because We Can tour in Brisbane the following week, I was okay with that. Dylan needed rest, so we snuck off back to our accommodation before he reached complete exhaustion.

Despite my best efforts and high hopes there had been no media interest in my fan story. There are millions of us out there, so I'm sure I had some stiff competition!

I put my disappointment aside as I got ready to attend the band's final show of the tour at Suncorp Stadium in Brisbane. I was meeting up with Paige and Kyla and my high school buddy Rachel Eddy, or Eddy as we called her. She and two of her friends Liv and Re had flown down from Darwin to attend the concert. All of us wore 'Chasing Jon' shirts and carried a fan banner that lit up with fairy lights.

I may not have succeeded in getting on Bon Jovi's radar, but I had so much support from the amazing people in my life. I was blessed. We grabbed some beers, took our seats, and enjoyed the show.

Me, Ronny and Chell

Our family home

Me and my babies

Working at Pink's Brisbane concerts with the Live Nation crew

CHAPTER ELEVEN

Chasing Jon

I was working away at Merthyr Law one morning, diligently entering safe custody items into the register, when an email notification popped up on the bottom of my computer screen. It was from the Backstage Bon Jovi fan club, and the subject line read:

'Runaway to NYC with Jon Bon Jovi!'

I opened the email eagerly, my excitement building with every word I read.

Unable to contain myself, I rushed over to Miki's office, directly across from mine, and in my best radio voice I announced,

'Join Jon Bon Jovi for an intimate acoustic performance at BB Kings, one of NYC's premier music venues!'

Miki looked up from her computer, about to say something. '–Including two nights' accommodation at the luxury Intercontinental in New York's Time Square, photo op with JBJ, after show party, autographed poster and an exclusive photo with the man, the legend that is JBJ!'

'I'm busy, Bizzjovi, get out!'

'Toots! This is the opportunity of a lifetime, the moment I have waited almost 30 years for!!'

She looked at me intently.

'When exactly is this opportunity of a lifetime taking place?'

'Next month,' I replied.

'Next month!'

'That's right, next month and I'm going to see if Ma wants to go with me.'

Miki was laughing.

'Good luck with that, there is no way Ma is going to agree to be part of your latest crazy scheme.'

'We shall see about that – and what are you talking about, Toots, you've agreed to a few haha!'

'Out out,' she said with an eye roll and a laugh as I departed, heading for my mother's office.

In Frannie's office I found her, as usual, surrounded by files and folders, her gaze fully focused on her computer screen, typing away with the radio playing in the background.

'Frannie, I think you are in need of an adventure,' I announced.

'What are you up to now Bizz?'

'I know you have always wanted to go to the United States, and I have found the perfect adventure for us, at an affordable price.'

'Bizz, I'm trying to work here.' Her gaze had returned to her computer screen.

'And you are amazing at your job, but there is more to life than work, Frannie, life is about memories and moments, so we are going to the Big Apple, New York City, to create the most amazing memories!'

She laughed.

'New York? What on earth are you on about?'

'Jon Bon Jovi is doing a Runaway tour at BB Kings in Times Square, it's a three-day event and it includes a meet and greet with the man himself!'

'When is it?'

'Next month.'

'NEXT MONTH! It's the end of the financial year and Steve doesn't like us having time off at the same time, let alone at short notice and at the end of the financial year.'

'I hear you, but this really is a once-in-a-lifetime trip and I think Steve will say yes. He loves a good adventure himself so will understand, I'm sure of it. Let's put in a request, and see?'

'I need time to think about this Bizz, let's talk about it later?'

Deciding I shouldn't push my luck, I agreed and left to try to get some work done, but my mind was going a million miles an hour. Not only would this event be a lifelong dream come true but could also be the opportunity to get my film on Jon's radar.

A month later, Frannie and I landed at LAX excited and ready for our adventure. Mum had never been to the US before, so I wanted her to experience Hollywood before we went to NYC.

I love Los Angeles. For me, it is the land for those with big dreams: a sprawling city of concrete highways, rolling hills, palm trees, blue skies, and beautiful beaches. The history of cinema is everywhere you look, the landmarks and the studios.

I had booked us four nights' accommodation at the historic Hotel Roosevelt right in the heart of Hollywood. Some of the world's biggest stars have stayed there, including Errol Flynn and Clark Gable. Marilyn Monroe called the Hollywood Oasis home for a couple of years.

Mum was captivated by the mix of old vintage style and new age glamour, as we adopted the movie star lifestyle, lazing poolside and sipping cocktails in the elegant Spare Room.

Determined to get the most out of the little time we had, we spent our days soaking up the Californian sunshine at some of my favourite LA locations, like Venice Beach and Santa Monica Pier. I took mum on a tour of Paramount Studios where our tour guide regaled us with stories of Lucille Ball and Desi Arnaz. We even caught a glimpse of David Duchovny leaving one of the sound stages, a real thrill for me as a mad *X-Files* fan.

As the tour and day ended, I captured a Kodak moment of my beautiful mum sitting by the fountain at the studio entrance. She looked like a young girl lost in deep thought, eyes full of wonder and beauty. I felt like I was seeing things for the first time through her eyes. I wondered what dreams she'd had for her life. The woman I knew had always put others before herself.

My mother, then 58, had already had her hips replaced three times each, which at times had affected her mobility, and mobility affects accessibility. I wondered if that is why she'd never travelled. My memories of mum are of a strong yet gentle woman who taught me to live with kindness, empathy, honesty and compassion.

Sensing my gaze, she turned and smiled, drawing us both back into the moment. We left our magical day at the studios behind and headed back to our hotel.

On our third day in LA we decided to go our separate ways. I had been invited to a BBQ at my friend Mikki's house and mum had decided to venture off alone on a bus tour of the Hollywood Hills to see the homes of the stars. I waved mum off before jumping in an uber to Mikki's, carrying a care package of her favourite Aussie items, including Tim Tams and Vegemite. It was nice to meet some of Mikki's LA crew. Like Mikki, some of them also worked in the music industry, and she asked me to tell everyone why I was visiting the States. 'Oh god,' I thought, 'they are going to think I'm mad!'

'Well aside from it being a lifelong dream come true to meet the legendary JBJ, I also plan to tell him I've written a feature film inspired by his music and give him one of the film's flyers.'

'So, you're going to just walk up to him and say that?' someone asked.

'First I'm going to give him a boxing kangaroo teddy I brou—'

Before I could finish the sentence there was a chorus of 'no no, no, you are not going to give a grown man a teddy, plenty of people there will, but you are not going to be one of them!'

'Why not?'

'Because you are going to meet him as a professional, you're a filmmaker remember, not just another fan.'

'I am so nervous I don't even know if I'm going to be able to speak let alone be professional,' I said. 'And I really hope I don't trip over or something, this man's music literally has been my saving grace throughout my life.'

'Tell them about your bus,' Mikki said.

I filled them in on some of the crazy events of the last few years. I left there that day with a far better plan than the one I had arrived with, thanks to the divine intervention of these seasoned roadies.

After five days of LA sunshine, we boarded another plane, ready for the final leg of our adventure and the realisation of a dream thirty years in the making. I had printed some film flyers and was determined to get on the radar of the man who had inspired it.

Mum and I were seated in different rows on this flight. I was next to a beautiful woman with striking silver hair and a personality as warm as the Californian sunshine. She immediately introduced herself as Paulette Osborne, a New Yorker heading home after a brief visit to LA, who was sincerely interested in why this Aussie girl and her mum were visiting the Big Apple.

I explained and was surprised to hear she was no stranger to the entertainment world. She'd done some modelling in recent years and had two sons who both had achieved success in film and television.

In what could only be described as fate, I discovered that Paulette lived in an apartment across the road from where mum and I were staying in Times Square. We fell into an easy conversation for the duration of the flight like we had known each other for years and exchanged our contact details in the cab we shared to our accommodation.

The InterContinental New York Times Square, is thirty-six storeys high with stunning views of the Manhattan skyline, Hudson River and Broadway. The room was stylish and spacious, with a large bathroom and bedding that had us sleeping like queens the moment our heads hit the pillows.

The following morning, I awoke to a message from Paulette inviting mum and I to join her and a friend to attend an episode taping of *The View* hosted by Whoopie Goldberg, we didn't hesitate to accept.

As we left our building by day, Frannie stood spellbound at the sight of a vibrant and bustling Manhattan. A melting pot of people and cultures, the familiar skyline and contemporary buildings complemented by the blast of horns from the famous yellow taxis.

'I cannot believe I am standing on 42nd Street, never in my life did I think I would see this in person', she said.

I'll remember that moment forever. It felt like we had swapped places; I was the one guiding my mother as, with childlike wonder, she took in every detail of a world she had only ever seen on the silver screen.

We met up with Paulette out front of her apartment building before we went to the ABC studios where the show was filmed. Today's episode was about dogs. Whoopi Goldberg on a stage full of dogs? It was very entertaining and, as they always say in showbiz, never work with children or animals.

Paulette and I remain firm friends to this very day. Who knew such a random encounter would be such a gift?

Later, mum and I went to see Lady Liberty in New York harbour. We hopped on the subway and headed down to Battery Park, near the Financial District and the Hudson River at the southern tip of Manhattan Island. With limited time, we didn't take the ferry to Liberty Island but picked up some giant chocolate-covered pretzels and sat by the river watching the Staten Island ferry going back and forth across the harbour in front of the historic statue.

Our backstage Bon Jovi experience was about to begin. First was an afternoon presentation with David Bergman, Jon Bon Jovi's tour photographer. He told us many stories of touring with the band. His recently released book *Work* has some of the most epic photos ever taken of Bon Jovi in concert. David's warmth and humour had us all spellbound and he gave us a look into the technical side of tour photography, his eye for capturing live movement as a result of his days of sport photography.

After the presentation, we were all invited to attend a welcome party at John's Pizzeria of Times Square, 'the most unique pizzeria in the world'. The old Gospel Tabernacle Church still has the original stained-glass ceiling that is made up of eight parts of equal size, just like a pizza.

As we lined up outside waiting for the venue to open, we got to talking with other excited fans from the JoviNation, many of whom had travelled from across the globe to meet their idol just like I had. I told them about my film and handed out flyers and we shared stories about what the band's music meant to us. I felt like I became part of a community that night. It was the first time in my life I had met people with the same mad passion for the band. I declared 'I have found my people' to my mother's great amusement. We met so many wonderful people as we danced the night away.

It was so great to see mum mingling and dancing without a care in the world in her sequined shirt and jeans. I remembered just how much she loved to dance.

The following morning there were dozens of notifications on my social media in response to my announcement the previous day that I was in NYC to meet JBJ. It was met with a tidal wave of support by countless friends. Will I get to talk to him? Will I get to tell him about my film? I was asking myself the same questions and my excitement was mixed with extreme nervousness now that the day was finally here.

It was also our final day in the Big Apple, so I took mum on a shopping trip to Macy's department store in Herald Square at 34th and Broadway. It's the largest department store in the United States, built in 1902. The sheer size and beauty of the building had mum in awe as she went in search of gifts to take home. No girl's shopping trip would be complete without the purchase of some new clothes and shoes, so we also shopped for ourselves until our feet hurt.

We finished our morning with an early lunch and a glass of Long Island iced tea in celebration of our adventure so far, and to calm the nerves I was feeling in anticipation of my imminent mission. How does one convey in a brief moment the impact one band's music has had on their entire life, especially when you know you are one of many. It had been such an amazing experience to meet so many loyal fans the night before, who understood the same deep devotion as we shared stories with one another. But the real impact of music is felt in those moments when you are alone and the lyrics become a friend, guiding you through moments where life is so fucking hard, or moments of pure joy.

I knew people back home were cheering me on but that also gave me feelings of added pressure to achieve something in this moment, rather than just enjoy it as a fan.

Hours later as we lined up outside B.B. King Blues Club & Grill, we were reacquainted with some of our new friends who had travelled from different corners of the globe, as well as other Aussies, and this was not their first backstage rodeo! We were ushered inside the famous venue that has presented some of the biggest names in all genres of live music, from Ray Charles to ZZ Top, as well as B.B. King himself, and of course, the one and only Jon Bon Jovi.

As we took our seats, we were told there would be the opportunity to ask questions during the evening.

'I know exactly what I'm going to ask if I get the chance,' I said.

'Do you want me to record you?'

'Hell no, I'm beyond nervous as it is, Frannie.'

Anticipation was building, and when JBJ finally appeared the room erupted in applause, wolf whistles and some 'I love you, Jon'. Jon sat down and began his acoustic performance. Questions were allowed in between every couple of songs.

I raised my hand along with a number of other people and to my complete surprise I was one of those selected to ask a question. I was sick with nerves as the man with the microphone whispered.

'Okay, you're next, I think Jon will be ready for another question after this song so stand up.'

As I stood on wobbly legs Jon continued on with another song and the man motioned for me to sit down again. This happened three times before I actually got to ask the question that I had rehearsed word for word in my mind, I just hoped the words would come out! I took a deep breath and with a shaky voice I asked.

'Hi Jon, I've heard that from a young age you were both driven and determined to carve out a successful career whilst always remaining true to your vision. That's not an easy thing to do in such a harsh industry and I'm wondering if there was a defining moment where you knew no matter what, you would remain true to you?'

I heard a whisper close by: 'That was a good question.'

Jon looked intently in my direction. I don't recall his response word for word because my heart was pounding so hard at this point it was like a drum beating, but the gist of it was that every step of his journey he'd celebrated his success: his first gig, his first stadium show, but as an artist you always strive to continue to create, to write the best song and see how that song is received.

Jon has talked often over the years of his humble beginnings growing up in Jersey in an Eastern European family that had migrated to the US, and of his early years selling newspaper subscriptions and working at a fast-food place whilst pursuing his single-minded focus to make and record music.

With an incredible will to succeed, he began playing in bars at sixteen with his parents' support and secured his first record contract at the age of twenty. He is still with that record company today. Bon Jovi has sold 120 million records worldwide and played to over 34 million fans, but for me, one of the things I admire most about JBJ is his service to others. This began with building housing for those in need before his wife Dorothea (his high school sweetheart) came up with the idea to help feed those they house.

This is how JBJ Soul Kitchen came about, a farm-to-table restaurant in Jersey with no prices on the menu. A place where all are welcome: those who can afford to pay do so by paying it forward for someone in need who will volunteer in return for their meal.

The biggest lesson I have taken from this rock star throughout my life is the importance of connection, whether through a song or by giving someone in need a hand up. His response to my question confirmed that he was who I believed him to be.

As the performance came to an end, we were asked to line up for our photo opportunity. Photos were to be taken in groups and my mother had graciously opted to sit it out so I could have my photo just with Jon, but also because she knew this was the moment I had to put my mission into motion and inform him of my film.

I decided the best opportunity to pull this off would be for me to go last, so I stood at the end of the line with the film's flyer in hand for what seemed an eternity before it was finally my moment to step forward and shake the hand of the man whose music had changed my life. With a confidence that belied the internal somersault of nerves in my gut, I stepped forward with outstretched hand and as he shook it I said:

'Hi, my name is Belinda, I'm a filmmaker from Australia. I've written a feature film inspired by your music and I would just like for you to check it out.'

I handed him a flyer as he said 'Okay, I'll check it out' and put the flyer in his pocket before putting his arm around me and we smiled for the photographer.

I walked off with legs like jelly, feeling like I might faint towards my mother who was proudly watching on.

With Jon's performance complete, mum and I stayed on for a little longer to mingle with the JoviNation before heading back to our apartment to try to get some sleep before our long journey home the following day. I was buzzing with the euphoria of achieving my lifelong dream of meeting JBJ, and also in a state of disbelief that I had actually successfully achieved my mission of getting my film on Jon's radar.

Mum and I at BB Kings in New York for our Runaway with Jon Bon Jovi experience

Finally meeting Jon Bon Jovi

Photo credit: Robert Fuzesi

Paulette and I at the View

Frannie at the fountain

CHAPTER TWELVE

Robbed and Rolled

I was having difficulty concentrating and retaining information. I had the memory of a goldfish, which frightened me.

One Friday afternoon, Courtney, Natalie, Jacqui and I returned to the office after a Friday lunch. I put my handbag in my office and wandered to the other end of the office to chat with Marie. When I returned my handbag was on my office chair and I couldn't find my purse anywhere.

After a thorough look, I thought maybe I'd accidentally left it where we had lunch. I informed the office manager Frannie that my purse was missing and that I was going back to see if I'd left it behind.

I hurried off, hoping someone may have handed it in. I couldn't see it anywhere, and checked with centre management, but nothing, so I returned to the office certain that I did not leave my bag on the chair. I always put it straight under my desk. Someone must have moved it.

We began a thorough search of the office and it wasn't long before Frannie found it in the back room, on top of the filing cabinet.

All my money was gone. I had only just withdrawn my cash for the week so $350 was missing.

We were in a state of disbelief. How could this have happened in the office? I knew, beyond a shadow of a doubt, that no one who worked there would take it, but anyone sneaking in would have to walk past reception and a heap of offices before getting to mine.

The only other entry point was the door at the back of the office where the purse had been found. The door was indeed unlocked.

'That door should always be locked; Steve is going to hit the roof.'

'Some asshole has entered a law firm in the middle of the day in Brisbane City, stolen cash from an office undetected, and left without anyone seeing anything!' I was getting more pissed off by the minute.

Back in Frannie's office she contacted our tech company and asked them to check the security camera footage for the afternoon.

I was too angry, stressed and shocked to do any work. I couldn't concentrate at all. News of the robbery had filtered down to the other end of the office, so I also had a steady stream of stunned workers turn up at my office door.

I wouldn't have to wait long before the footage from the security camera was sent through.

Courtney, Jacqui and I huddled around mum's desk to see her computer screen. We were all speechless. An older male with grey hair walked into the back filing area with my purse, took out the cash, put it on the filing cabinet and let himself out the back door.

The audacity. I felt sick to my stomach and, for the first time, I allowed myself to think two words that I really hate:

'Why me?'

This piece of shit targets *me* and takes *my* hard-earned money. It felt so personal at the time, but it was just a random crime.

Frannie called the police, reported the robbery, and told them we had footage. They didn't have the time or resources to come out to investigate petty crime and I felt like I had been robbed twice: first by a criminal, second by the system that, yet again, had let me down. I was becoming jaded.

Friday afternoon drinks were a weekly thing in our office. We'd finish work an hour early and congregate in the boardroom to wind down from the week.

I would usually have one or two glasses of wine, but still feeling really shaken by the afternoon's events, two glasses became a bottle, maybe two. I really can't remember.

At some point Frannie gave me a cab charge to get home and one of the lawyers helped me into a cab to make sure I got home safely. The rest of the night is a blur. By the time I reached the house I had lost the capacity to walk and to reason. The following description of events has been provided by Miki and Huddo who have recounted them to me on numerous occasions.

I got out of the taxi without paying and rolled down the embankment across from our home, which was on a hill. The taxi driver, concerned about my welfare and receiving his payment, drove to the police station and returned with the police. The police went into my bag to find my ID and address, which of course was across the road.

One of them stayed with me and the other knocked on our front door. Poor Hudson got the fright of his life when he answered the door. A policeman asked:

'Is your mum Belinda Adams?'

'Yes.'

'We've got her outside, highly intoxicated.'

Knowing now that this was not a life-and-death situation but rather one of great humiliation he replied.

'I'll just get my sister.'

Nicely hand-balling the shame job. Miki and D kindly paid the taxi driver so that I wouldn't be charged with evasion of fare, then they helped me into the house.

I awoke late the following morning feeling like death and made a mad dash to the toilet to heave my guts up. What little was left to heave. I had no recollection of the previous night's events and wished it could have stayed that way but hearing my movements, Miki appeared at my bedroom door.

'So, you're finally alive again. Remember much about last night?'

'I remember getting robbed.'

She started to recount the events for me and Hudson chimed in with his condemnation at me for having our roles reversed. I wasn't up for this trip down memory lane.

'Everybody out,' I whispered and shrunk under the covers, mortified. Hudson was right, my kids shouldn't be answering the door to police bringing me home drunk and disorderly.

Later, Miki's condemnation became compassion. She brought me a feed of Kentucky to cure my hangover and asked me about the details of the robbery.

I filled in the gaps, including the lack of investigation, and she suggested I go into Erin Brockovich mode, as usual, and solve it myself. I decided that was precisely what I would do.

On Monday morning I asked Steve's permission to share some screenshot images of the robber on social media, hoping someone would recognise him. Steve agreed. He wanted the guy caught as much as I did and was just as angry at the brazenness of the theft.

I uploaded the pictures asking people to share. I was blown away by how many people shared and by the countless messages of support. It seems when we are shown the worst of humanity, we are also shown the best.

A few days later I received a message from one of the soccer mums I had befriended during Miki's soccer days, informing me a contact in her friends list knew who the robber was. He worked at a prison and the man was a regular inmate there. He kindly sent through his details, and we were able to go to the police with all the evidence they needed to charge the guy. The mystery was solved!

CHAPTER THIRTEEN

I Grieved

The kids all settled into a routine in our new home. Hudson was doing well in his new school, had a nice group of friends and only had to walk to the end of the street to get there. Miki had decided to leave Merthyr Law as she had been offered a job at an accounting firm full-time so had made the decision to leave uni. She and D wanted to travel, and they also contributed to the house by paying board. Now that Dylan had his licence again, he had gone back to work for Earthpro, for whom he'd worked for briefly just before he started his landscaping business. In fact, working for them had prompted the idea of starting his own business. He was still dealing with many invisible barriers, but for the first since his accident, he was somewhat independent.

As for me, I was sliding into an abyss. It felt like more had happened in my life in the preceding five years than in the previous twenty. I was tired. Not the kind of tired that sleep can fix.

I felt like I was sitting outside my own body, watching a showreel of the previous year's events. I was so overwhelmed that I didn't want to leave the house. Negative thoughts constantly invaded my mind. I had invested time and resources in writing something that was too close to my own experience to be any good and had come to believe my screenplay was shit.

Worst of all, others had invested in me as well, and I felt like a fraud. During my 'you can die at any moment' phase, I'd flipped from lacking confidence to being overconfident. It was becoming clear that I'd overestimated my own limitations.

Who the hell flies to the opposite side of the world and tells one of the world's biggest rock stars they've written a feature film inspired by his music? Sure, I'd written a screenplay – numerous drafts – but it wasn't ready for the screen. It still needed so much work.

I was only just starting to understand how hard making a film was, and the odds of making it from script to screen. Yet here I was promoting a film that I was now realising may never get made.

I was making mistakes at work. First these were small mistakes, but one day I accidentally stamped a legal document with the posted stamp instead of the safe custody entry form. This was not a minor error, and I no longer trusted myself.

I left my job and my business partnership, my head full of doubt and my heart full of pain. The experiences of the past five years had made me lose faith in the systems I'd trusted and which I thought were in place to protect us.

At my farewell do I told Steve that my greatest realisation this year was that 'Everybody is full of shit', even me, because I felt like I had no idea what I was doing.

I knew I needed help, so I made an appointment to see a counsellor that came highly recommended. It was my first time seeing a counsellor and I wasn't sure what to expect.

At our first session, I gave a basic rundown of the past few years' events. It took up most of the session. The counsellor probed a little deeper about the time following Dylan's accident, brain injury and recovery. She said something which was so powerful to me.

'What you have experienced with your son is called ambiguous grief. You have been grieving someone who is still alive. You still have your son, but his personality has changed and so has his life, all your lives.'

Finally, someone understood. And with understanding came permission to feel the things that I had tried so hard to suppress because, as everyone liked to tell me, I was so lucky because Dylan was still here. But I also had a right to feel the loss of who my son was before his accident.

These last few years had been fucking hard. I had wonderful support, but I had to go through so much of the experience on my own. The counsellor also explained that, when we are dealing with extreme trauma, our bodies can go into fight or flight mode. Initially I had to fight, but then I went into flight, which explained running off on road trips and to the US on a whim.

During these phases our bodies run on adrenaline until we hit adrenal fatigue, then the body shuts down. Which is where I was at now. I wasn't going crazy and, if anything, she said, the fact it had taken two and half years to reach this point was a testament to my strength.

I began, finally, to release everything I'd held inside since my divorce five years earlier. I wasn't just feeling the ambiguous grief for Dylan, but for all the loss which had happened over such a short period of time. I grieved for the end of my marriage in 2009, when the man to whom I had dedicated twenty years of my life discarded me so easily.

There's a weird process you go through after divorce as you try to rediscover who you are again outside of a partnership, including losing some of your friends from your married days. I think some friends feel they need to take sides and others don't understand the process of rediscovery of being single for the first time in twenty years. As you change, so, too, do your friendships.

I grieved for the loss of my Grandma Addie, a pillar of strength throughout my life. We'd moved in with grandma after my parents divorced and she had bought herself a little caravan, parked it in the backyard, and moved into it to give us her home.

She was the strongest woman I knew, raised on a wheat and sheep farm. From the age of ten, Grandma became her father's offsider, milking cows, feeding the animals, and helping mark the lambs.

She also helped with the harvesting of the wheat. Her dad drove the tractor, and she sat on the 'Big E' Harvester lifting the combs up and down to catch the wheat. Drought and depression drove them off the farm in 1937. They moved to Hay where she finished her education at the Presentation Sisters, then took a job as a clerk at Meakes & Wheeler's general store.

The family moved to Sydney when her brother contracted polio, to be near him at the Alexandra Hospital for Children. Grandma took a job in real estate doing clerical work, advertising, and research. During the war years she also volunteered with the National Emergency Services, RSL Women's Auxiliary and the American Red Cross. She met my grandpa Michael at a dance at the YMCA when he was on leave from the army, and they married in 1947. They would eventually move to Michael's hometown of Broken Hill where he returned to work on the mines. This is where they raised their seven children, four sons and three daughters, and how I came to be born in Broken Hill.

Grandpa passed away in 1980 when I was just six years old, but grandma continued to fill her life with rich experiences, taking up oil painting, singing with the Philharmonic Society and travelling to Europe when she was sixty-five. She continued to volunteer in numerous charities and worked in an aged care facility until she retired, sold her house, and moved into one herself.

My grandma taught me resilience, kindness and grace, she taught me to turn pain into purpose, to lift others as you rise, that laughter truly is the best medicine and gentleness is your greatest strength. She taught me the importance of community and to always help others when you can. Grandma passed away in February 2011 and we didn't make it back to Broken Hill in time to say goodbye. I missed our chats, I missed her laugh and I missed her wisdom. I couldn't even imagine visiting Broken Hill without sitting in her home sharing a cuppa, a glass of port or a piece of ginger, which were her favourites.

I had called on her spirit to guide me so many times throughout Dylan's recovery, especially during those early days when he was still in a coma when I would ask grandma to help guide Dylan back to us. I kept grandma's perfume and powder which I still have to this day. On days when I find myself missing her most, I smell her perfume and I feel her warmth surround me still.

Not long after I lost grandma, we discovered my faithful furry friend Memphis Maree had cancer. Memphis was a little dog with a big personality. She could sit and roll over on command and she is the only dog I have ever known who could brush her teeth with a toothbrush when instructed. She was my shadow, my best friend and the one constant in a time of so much change. But she was suffering, so I made the heart-wrenching decision to have her put to sleep. I took a week off work so I could spend every moment of her final week with her. We went to the park every day; we went for ice cream, and she ate steak for dinner every night. On her final day I dressed her in her Bon Jovi shirt, which I had bought from the Bon Jovi website years earlier. Instead of a dagger through the heart, it had a bone and said Bone Jovi.

Dylan drove us to the vet and my beautiful neighbour Maryanne came along for moral support. I will never forget Memphis hanging her head out the car window like she was off on an adventure, while tears streamed down my face. These were our final moments together. I held her tight until she closed her eyes for the last time. To me, pets are family, they give us unconditional love and joy.

I had Memphis cremated in her Bon Jovi shirt and plan to have her ashes scattered with mine when my time comes. I still haven't been able to get another pet, but I did buy a dog for Miki a few years later. I love and adore Dante, but he is without a doubt Miki's dog.

I grieved for Ron and Jase; Jase had recently been killed in a horrific workplace accident. It was almost impossible to comprehend that these two guys who were so full of life and character were both taken so suddenly and within such a short space of time of one another. Ronny had been a pillar of strength during my divorce and after Dylan's accident. Jase had always made me laugh with his mischievous nature. Ron and Shell had done most of the work in organising Dylan's twentieth birthday party up at the soccer club where Shell ran the canteen even long after Miki and Sarah stopped playing.

I have so many treasured memories of family barbecues, nights out and, best of all, nights sitting around the Campbell's pool or on the roof with a beer in hand. To this day I can still hear Ronny say:

'What are you doin here? You think you're goin up to sit on my roofus eh?' XXXX beer in hand, wearing his concreter's thongs.

He was so proud of his family, and they loved him to bits. I couldn't fathom the pain Candy, Brendan and Sarah must have felt at this time losing their father and a brother.

I grieved for the loss of our home, and the community we had built around that home, and the security of having roots and support. I grieved for Dylan's loss of self, loss of friends and loss of independence, for Mikaela and Hudson's loss of innocence and time with me. I grieved for myself. I finally stopped running and sat in my grief.

CHAPTER FOURTEEN

You Couldn't Make This Shit up

A year flew by.

I'm not even sure what I did during that year. I couldn't read, couldn't watch television, and didn't socialise. I'd stopped working on my screenplay, had ended my business partnership, and withdrew from the world. I did meet a man during this time when I was at my most vulnerable, but more about that later.

The last remnant of my stable life went when I was involved in a pile up on the motorway during a freak storm. The rainstorm came out of nowhere and bucketed down, causing water to pool on the highway. I noticed there were multiple vehicles breaking in front of me and slammed my foot on the brake. My car aquaplaned straight into the back of the car in front, making me the fourth car in the collision.

In a state of shock, I noticed smoke billowing out from beneath the hood. I surveyed the scene. It was too dangerous to try to get out of the vehicle – I was in the centre lane and cars were still flying past me on either side, and there was very low visibility. I'm not sure how long I sat in the vehicle, slowly moving all my body parts to make sure I was not injured, before a tow truck appeared. The front of the car was crumpled like a piece of cardboard. I knew it was going to be a write-off.

The kind young towie helped me into the cab of his truck and loaded up my car on the back tray.

While I waited for the insurance cheque to come through, I managed to find a little Daihatsu on Gumtree for $1000. The body looked a bit shabby, door handles were half broken off, and I discovered some cigarette butts rammed into the air conditioning vents, but mechanically it seemed okay. The car looked a little like I felt, so I decided to keep her and hold onto the insurance cheque when it came through for more pressing issues.

Miki was soon to marry her childhood sweetheart and they were about to purchase their first home, due to settle the same time our lease expired, a week before their wedding date. Without their board I wouldn't be able to afford to rent, so they offered to put me up while I got back on my feet.

Dylan decided to move into his dad's. Paul was living in a house on a large block of land near the landfill where he worked. Dylan would have an entire side of the large house to himself, as well as space to tinker and build, as he liked to do.

Hudson and I moved with Miki and D from Brisbane City to Tanah Merah, in between Brisbane and the Gold Coast. The greatest joy at this time was preparing for my baby girl's wedding day. Some said she was too young to marry, but I trusted her heart. She was wise beyond her years and, unlike me and my mother before me, she was marrying not because she was pregnant, but because she was deeply in love.

They were the embodiment of what a partnership should and could be. They had individual goals that they each embraced and encouraged in the other, and they had shared goals also. I was in my forties and still had not experienced a partnership like they had. I haven't to this day. What more does a parent want for a child than a partner who loves and protects them as fiercely as you do? So, they had my blessing!

The months leading up to the wedding spent with Miki and Sar Bear, who was matron of honour, were precious. Miki had a strong sense of self and it shone on her wedding day. They were married on the beach at Mooloolaba.

Miki wore a stunning white gown with a pair of Vans sneakers she'd decorated with glitter. I was honoured to walk her down the aisle with her father. Paul and I walked either side, arm in arm with Miki, until she reached the wooden arch and dreamcatcher where her husband-to-be stood waiting.

I took my place with the family and friends who were gathered on the beach. I looked at her brothers, standing beside D, cute as a button in their groomsmen suits. I realised how grown up they all were and was hit with a tidal wave of emotion.

The wedding behind us, I needed another reason to get out of bed in the morning. I needed to be outdoors, and to do something that didn't involve using my brain because I still didn't trust it to work properly. I was still struggling to retain information and concentrate.

D was working for Paul at the Rochedale landfill and mentioned that he was often looking for extra casuals to pick up rubbish from the perimeter of the property. I allowed myself to be vulnerable and approached my ex-husband to ask if he could give me a few days casual work. He agreed to a trial. If it worked out, on both sides, he would give me ongoing casual work.

I dragged myself out of bed on the first day and managed to arrive on time. I was wearing a high-vis shirt with 'Dylan' embroidered across the front, which Dylan had kindly leant me. I wondered how the operators would feel about the foreman's ex-wife working at the site, but my fears were completely unfounded. I was welcomed with open arms by the small team.

Paul was very professional, greeting me and giving me the rundown on my job: driving a little truck around the base of the landfill and collecting all the rubbish that wind gusts had blown out of the dump site. I was given a claw-like apparatus to pick up the rubbish, some big hessian bags to fill, and a quick tour of the site. Then I was handed the keys to the truck.

I put my headphones in and went to work. It was eye-opening to see how much plastic goes to landfill. In a cluster of rubbish that had collected around the base of a tree, I spotted a medium-sized foam ball. 'Wilson my friend,' I said, thinking of a film, as I so often did. I picked my new mascot up with the claw and placed it on the truck behind the cab.

By the end of the day my hand hurt from clenching the claw lever in and out all day, and I was physically exhausted from walking, but I felt like I had accomplished something. Not only for myself: it felt good to be cleaning up for Mother Earth. I enjoyed being outside by myself all day, though it would take some time to get used to the stench that rose from the dump site.

Paul was eager to hear how I felt about my first day on the job. I think I surprised us both when I said I was keen to return. I knew I would adjust to the smell and the physicality of the job in no time at all. The position was perfect for me and, for now, was all I was able to handle.

Dylan was going out more to socialise with his friends. I was excited, if a little nervous, when he said he was seeing a girl that he wanted me to meet. It was two years since his accident, but he was still dealing with invisible barriers, and I wondered if a relationship would be too much for him. I met them for lunch at the local shopping centre and was relieved to find that Cindy (not her real name) was a kind, smart young lady who seemed to care for Dylan.

So, I was shocked to my core a week later when Dylan told me that Cindy was pregnant with their baby. Say what? Dylan confirmed that they had only been seeing each other for two weeks, but I decided not to press for any further information. Something was not adding up.

The following day, a proud and excited Dylan told me he and Cindy had been for an ultrasound. He sent me a photo with the caption, 'Your first grandchild'.

I zoomed in on the image. The gestational age of the baby was 6 weeks and 3 days. There was no chance that Dylan was the father, and Cindy knew it and was willingly deceiving someone she knew was vulnerable. My initial reaction was anger, then deep sadness. I was going to have to tell Dylan the truth, break his heart all over again, and I had to do it asap. I messaged him straight back and invited him to dinner that night at Miki's.

A proud Dylan arrived a few hours later, bubbling over with excitement about becoming a father, something he didn't think would be possible after his accident. I felt sick to my stomach. How on earth was I going to break this news to him? I pulled up the photo of the ultrasound on my phone and explained gently to Dylan that he could not possibly be the father of the baby. He had only been seeing Cindy for two weeks.

'But Mum, Cindy wants to be with me. I'm not supposed to tell you this, but Cindy's mum Angelica (not her real name) took us shopping and paid a deposit on some wedding rings but don't worry, it's not a real wedding, we are just going to an office.'

What the actual fuck!!! I fought with every fibre to remain calm.

'Dylan, my darling, that IS the real part of a wedding, the part that ties you together legally. I am so sorry to say this to you, but they have misled you with lies!'

I could see Dylan slowly processing this information, grateful that he trusted me implicitly and knew that I would never lie to him. I insisted he give me Cindy's number and suggested he let me handle the situation from there, but he was trying to regain his independence and wanted to speak to Cindy himself. I had no choice but to reluctantly agree.

The queasiness stayed with me as I waved Dylan goodbye, feeling like he was being fed to the wolves. It was so hard to balance protecting him, knowing how vulnerable he was, and allowing him to regain his independence by advocating for himself. Feeling heartbroken and helpless, I had no choice but to wait for Dylan to call me.

It was a few hours that felt more like days before Dylan called and filled me in. Cindy had conceded that, to her surprise, perhaps the baby wasn't his after all. But he was the man she wanted to be with, and she still wanted to marry him.

I had to tread carefully. I needed Dylan to see this clearly without my influence, so I suggested that it was too soon for marriage, and that he inform Cindy I was his legal guardian, so he needed my permission to get married. I felt it would be easier for him to pass the responsibility to me if needed.

The following day, while I was collecting rubbish at the landfill, I received a call from Dylan who, terrified, had locked himself in the bathroom at Paul's house, next door to the landfill.

'Mum, they are here at the house, and Angelica is threatening me and you! I've locked myself in the bathroom, can you come quickly.'

I called Paul who sped from the other side of the landfill in his work ute and drove us through the connecting gate to the house. Angelica's car pulled away from the house as we screeched to a halt out the front and raced inside. Dylan was still locked in the bathroom.

'It's okay my darling, you can come out. They're gone.'

Dylan emerged timidly from the bathroom. He looked emotionally devastated. I asked what had happened and what threats had been made.

'I told Cindy I couldn't get married without your permission and you wouldn't give it. Angelica got angry and said she needed Cindy to get married before her father found out about the baby. She demanded I pay her for the wedding ring deposit. She also left a message on my phone about you.'

'What on earth could she have threatened me about?'

Dylan played me the voicemail. 'Dylan, I know you're in there. I'm going to report your mother to Centrelink for ripping off the system, claiming to be a carer. People like you hide behind curtains, and I want my money back.'

WOW does not even begin to describe the disbelief of the moment! They were vultures, pecking at the pieces of the life Dylan was trying to put back together.

'That's it, we are going to the police station and there won't be a curtain big enough in Australia for that evil bitch to hide behind.'

Dylan and I jumped in his car and we drove to the local copshop. Dylan cranked the tunes, and Bon Jovi's 'Wanted Dead or Alive' blasted through the speakers. We looked at each other and broke up laughing, even though the situation was far from humorous.

Dylan and I relayed the crazy events that had taken place the preceding few days to one of the police officers on duty then played him the audio message from Angelica.

'Do I look like I'm getting a free ride? For the record, I am not currently on any carer payment, I am working part-time for my ex-husband picking up rubbish at the landfill, sorry if I smell. I can't work full-time because I need to be available for these kinds of situations. My son's disability is invisible, so getting assistance is very difficult because most of the time it's hard enough just being believed, as proven by this incident.'

The officer asked Dylan for Cindy's phone number and he called her. She admitted to everything and was instructed that she and her mother were not to contact us again or they could be charged with trespassing and harassment.

Dylan was again doubting his own ability to judge people. I was left doubting the future of humanity. These people had tried to take advantage of someone with a good heart, who had already lost so much.

A very proud mother of the bride with my beautiful Miki

Miki and D getting married

CHAPTER FIFTEEN

School's Out

Every bad experience seemed to be countered with a good one.

There are amazing people in this world, who make it a better place just by being in it. One such person is Warren Lindsay, Dylan's supervisor at Earthpro where he had been working as a dump truck driver.

Dylan felt comfortable enough with Warren to be completely honest about his brain injury so, when it became apparent that long hours as a heavy machine operator was not good for him, he shared his concerns about the headaches and back pain resulting from existing injuries.

Without hesitation, Warren moved Dylan to another role in site maintenance. Dylan thrived in this new position, until the company was sold. Then, due to downsizing, Dylan no longer had a job and Warren left to travel Australia with his family.

It was back to the drawing board again, trying to find a career for Dylan that would enable him to do meaningful work and move forward with his life.

Huddo was about to graduate from high school, and I felt like I had missed out on a large portion of his high school years. Despite the challenges, Huddo knuckled down and improved all his grades. At graduation he was recognised with the EEE Excellence Award, a Student Award for Learning, Respect and Cooperation: for consistent co-operative effort, respectful behaviour, and satisfactory achievement across all subjects.

Huddo also received the Award for Excellence, for high achievement across a range of subjects. He channelled the life experiences, dealt him at such a young age, into the ambition to carve out a career in justice. We were super proud when he enrolled at TAFE to study for a Crime and Justice Certificate and was then accepted into QUT to study a Bachelor of Justice.

I was now working for my dear friend and ex–Merthyr Law co-worker Marie Sheehy at her new law firm, Calvados-Woolf Lawyers. She and her partner Luke had decided to open dual firms, one at Upper Mount Gravatt, the other in Fortitude Valley. Miki and I again found ourselves in the same workplace, though I was in Fortitude Valley and she at Mount Gravatt.

I'd been nervous about returning to a high-paced administrative position and wasn't finding it easy. I was still a long way from my previous capacity for mental focus. Marie was aware of this and didn't overload me.

She also supported my personal projects, and invested in the recording of another little song I wrote called 'I'm Awkward' which was performed by my Miki chicki.

The irony was that the song was inspired by my dear children giving me stick about my sometimes awkward nature and here was Miki singing an anthem about acceptance.

I collaborated with Ric Parker from R&D Records to co-write the song. He produced the song and composed the music, and also played every instrument on the track. I brought Dylan, Huddo and Frannie in to join me as the clappers.

The bus went on another epic journey when I drove to the Crystal Castle in northern NSW with family, friends, and my trusty cameraman Jacques. We shot the music video at this magical sanctuary in Byron Bay's hinterland, surrounded by some of the biggest crystals on earth.

I had been described as being a little 'woo woo' the previous few years, exploring meditation and natural forms of healing, so I was determined the video reflects the lyrics of embracing your life and being proud of your woo woo!

Verse 1.

When someone tells me never

I'm more determined than ever.

To be awkward, a dork, eat my ice-cream with a fork.

Dot my I's and cross my T's, do anything I please,

Make a wish, catch a fish, maybe eat a scorpion....

Chorus

The journey of life is sugar and spice.

Roll the dice, take a chance and dance.

Dance naked under the moon and dance in the rain,

This moment will never come again.

Dance like a tree, buzz like a bee, spread your wings

fly and be free.

I'm Awkward!

Verse 2.

Cross the world to see a bear, catch a taxi from nowhere.

Swim with crocs, wear odd socks, jungle surfing upside

down.

Bareback ride a horse on the beach,

My phone's ringing but I can't reach.

Bronson look out for that tree!

Chorus

The journey of life is sugar and spice.

Roll the dice, take a chance and dance.

Dance naked under the moon and dance in the rain,

This moment will never come again.

Dance like a tree, buzz like a bee, spread your wings

fly and be free.

I'm Awkward!

Verse 3.

Buy a bus and take a ride, what's on the other side

See a frog race, don't feel out of place.

Swim in a waterfall, I see bubbles, I'm in trouble.

Swim fast, get out, don't muck about.

Try to shout but the words won't come out.

Oh wait, it's okay, it's only a turtle.

Draw whiskers on your friend's face.

Chorus

The journey of life is sugar and spice.

Roll the dice, take a chance and dance.

Dance naked under the moon and dance in the rain,

This moment will never come again.

Dance like a tree, buzz like a bee, spread your wings

fly and be free.

I'm Awkward!

Dylan was still struggling with the notion of self-acceptance post–brain injury. He still yearned for life to be as it was before his accident and felt without direction as he tried to find a suitable job.

I suggested that we may need to apply for disability services so that he would be formally recognised as having a disability. If he was in the system and his barriers were understood, they could assist in finding him suitable employment.

We had no idea what a difficult and lengthy process this would be. All the application forms seemed to ask questions relevant to a physical disability. Dylan could bathe and dress himself, although sometimes he needed to be reminded to. He had ongoing neuro fatigue, severe headaches and trouble regulating his emotions. This affected his ability to deal with conflict in a reasonable way. He also struggled to regulate his temperature and would sweat excessively at times. These were just a few of the challenges he was living with, though they were not visible, so difficult to prove.

It would take us a year to finally gain access to disability services. This was a big turning point for Dylan. He found the perfect job working at the very hospital where he recovered, as a wardsmen in environmental services. He was super proud to wear the Queensland Government uniform and work in a supported environment where he was able to also support others. Along with his natural empathy and kindness was an understanding of what it's like to be a long-term patient with a serious illness. He could offer hope when it felt there was none.

Hudson at his graduation

Miki in the recording studio with Ric Parker recordng I'm Awkward

CHAPTER SIXTEEN

Seismic Life

It was a crisp autumn morning in April 2017 as Miki and I rushed to the bus stop for our morning commute to work. I love this time of year, when the long hot days of summer are replaced by cool morning winds, shorter days, and the autumn hues of orange and brown. To me there is something healing about seeing the trees shedding their leaves. It brings a quiet contemplation about what I needed to shed from my own life.

I glanced at Miki sitting beside me on the bus reading her book. I felt overwhelming pride. The beautiful, strong, intelligent young woman sitting before me had carried so much on her young shoulders over the preceding years, including me at times. I needed to get out of her home, and to do that I needed to earn more than a three-day-a-week administration wage. Dylan had regained his independence with a job he loved, and I needed to regain mine. This would, in turn, give Miki hers. Although we could never fully understand the trauma Dylan had experienced, I was becoming increasingly aware of the shared family trauma of accompanying him on his journey.

Another one of my crazy ideas started to form. I had begun working on the bus conversion to motorhome and needed to get it back on the road. The next mission for the bus was starting to take shape: a trip around Australia to raise awareness of brain injury and to distribute vital resources and information. I needed to be a beacon of hope to others affected by brain injury, at a time when it can feel like there is none.

My thoughts were interrupted when Miki kissed me on the cheek and whispered, 'Have a good day, mum,' and got off at the next stop. She was working two jobs, one in customer service at Goodlife Gym and the second doing legal administration at the law firm. I wished Miki a good day too and waved as she got off the bus. Ideas were racing through my mind as the bus hurtled down the busway towards the city.

Later, at my desk, morning coffee in hand ready to begin another day, one thing became clear. If I had any hope of doing a national tour in my bus I was going to need to earn at least double the money so I could support myself financially on the road.

My computer whirred to life and began running through its usual morning checks while I sent a wish to the universe:

Dear universe, I need a job where I can earn a high income in a short timeframe so I can drive my bus around Australia to raise awareness and funds for brain injury, it would be greatly appreciated if you could please send me a sign of where to look, Belinda.

An hour or so later my phone vibrated on my desk, signaling a new message. I saw Buzz's name and I picked up the phone, eager to know what he would be messaging me about. 'Hey Bizz', I read, 'would you be interested in going out for a hitch on a seismic exploration crew? We are short of a few people for the next job. Need to know ASAP.'

I didn't know what the job entailed except that it required travel to remote locations, and that survey teams would lay out equipment that reads energy waves to form a geological picture of the area. Holy crap. I didn't know if I had what it takes physically, mentally, or emotionally to go out bush on a seismic crew, working and living away from home. I would earn double what I was at the time, and I had just asked the universe for a sign an hour earlier, so clearly I was meant to do this.

'I'm interested,' I texted back. 'Can you send me more information?'

'The crew is heading out in about two weeks, would need to get you in for a Coal Board Medical and safety inductions asap.'

'Okay, I'm in!'

I felt my old friend fear, trying to creep back. What on earth have I gotten myself into now I wondered. Feel the fear and do it anyway, I thought.

I sat in the doctor's office on my lunch break, awaiting my Coal Board Medical, a mandatory health assessment for miners that identifies respiratory issues.

The door opened and a doctor in his mid-thirties ushered me into the examination room. He asked me a heap of questions about my medical history then did tests for hearing, sight, respiratory system and flexibility.

The flexibility tests were especially challenging in the narrow skirt I wear to work: the doctor stretched my legs from one direction to the next and I had trouble not laughing. The most challenging was the spirometry test, where you have to blow into a machine until you almost pass out (my description). It measures how much air you can breathe in and out of your lungs.

Passing a Coal Board Medical is a requirement for all coal miners in Australia. Even though I wasn't actually going to be mining, we were searching for deposits of oil, gas and coal seams. Having grown up in a mining town, I accepted mining as part of everyday life and was just beginning to understand how politically charged it was. But the bus tour aside, I was barely making ends meet and, now that Dylan had regained his independence, I needed to get back on my feet too.

On the first day of my first hitch, I was up bright and early even though for half the night I was unable to sleep. As Miki drove me to the company workshop in Sumner Park, I was fighting back tears and crippling anxiety. I wondered if I'd made the right decision. For all that I had learned about fear, it still didn't stop the feeling. We don't always see fear in others, just as others don't see it in us, because at times we keep it hidden behind a front of false confidence.

I would feel the fear and do it anyway, and with familiarity comes confidence. Miki knew I was hanging on by a thread emotionally so tried to lift my mood with her bubbly chatter.

She pulled up in front of the workshop where a group of men were milling around wearing well-worn, high-vis uniforms and boots. They seemed at ease with one another, like a group of old friends reunited.

I glanced down at my brand-new uniform and boots, never worn, and shook my head. 'I feel like a kid on my first day of school', I said to Miki. She tried to stifle a giggle. I wonder how this looked to her. I couldn't imagine my own mother going from working in a law firm to heading off out bush with a bunch of blokes. It made me giggle myself.

'You ready?'

'Nope, but let's do this.'

I stepped out of the car. Miki helped get my suitcase out of the boot, hugged me goodbye and drove off. I took a deep breath in and walked into the workshop, heading straight for the safe and familiar sound of Buzz's voice.

I was given a mandatory drug test and had to blow in the breath machine before being handed the safety equipment

I'd require. I was then assigned a fob that I'd need to use when driving any of the vehicles to monitor my behaviour in the car. Breaches like speeding and not wearing seatbelts are recorded and sent to the employer and the company.

I was given a 'Take 5' booklet to fill out each time we began a new task. This was to identify risks in the field. It was quite a daunting initiation into a world that is highly regulated. I understood the need for safety – in Broken Hill a miners' memorial tells the stories of the many miners who lost their lives – but the process made one feel like a crim.

After everyone had passed all the mandatory tests, we gathered for a toolbox meeting. Buzz instructed the crew on convoy logistics then, giving me a quick squeeze, paired me up with industry veteran Wayno.

'You'll be right,' he whispered.

We hit the road in a convoy of 4X4s and trucks to Chinchilla for my first hitch. Wayno put me at ease instantly with his friendly banter and stories about the love of his life and their brood of kids. His love for them was obvious. The drive to Chinchilla from the workshop would take approximately four hours with one required stop along the way.

We pulled into the service station at Jondaryan for a quick lunch break and reached our destination by early afternoon. The accommodation, I was surprised to find, was quite luxurious. My room had a large, comfortable queen size bed, flat screen TV, desk and modern décor.

I unpacked my bags and was settling in when Wayno knocked on my door and insisted I come join the crew for a beer outside in the BBQ area before dinner.

'We don't bite,' he said.

I worked up the courage to join them, never comfortable in big group settings. I descended the stairs from my second-floor apartment and saw a familiar face, my old friend Bolly, who'd had driven my bus across the outback. He greeted me with a warm hug and invitation to sit with him at dinner which eased my nerves immensely.

After dinner most of the crew gathered again outside in the BBQ area for a few beers. There was real camaraderie amongst them. I said a shy goodnight as I passed by quickly on my way back to my room, determined to get a good night's sleep.

After another restless night I rose early to meditate. I was one of the first in the restaurant to eat breakfast and to pack my lunch and snacks for the day. I was impressed by the wide range of foods and chose a healthy salad with cold meat, and fruit to keep me fuelled through the day.

I learned we had to do a morning pre-start on our vehicles and fill up the 20 L water coolers then strap them to the back of each vehicle, so we had enough water to keep us hydrated in the field all day.

Next, at the toolbox meeting, we were allocated our positions and teams for the job. I was in the back crew with

Owie whom I warmed to straight away. Owie had an infectious chuckle and wore concreters' thongs. Petey, Kenny and Miles (Miles was at my induction and green like me) were also on the back crew. Miles was young with a happy disposition. The other three men were slightly older than me and had years of experience on the job. Their acceptance and kindness made everything easier.

The back crew were responsible for picking up the cables and geophones after the line had been shot. The front crew laid the cables and kicked in the geophones before a vibroseis truck drove the line, dropping a big plate that would vibrate the earth and send a frequency through the geophones. The cables were like long thick extension cords that we needed to roll up in a circular motion, then place it between our legs so we could clip the end toggles together. The geophones were hooked one by one onto a big metal hanger, then both pieces of equipment were placed back next to the survey peg markers for collection by the spread trucks.

Driving the spread trucks was regarded as prestigious because you got to spend half the time in the Ute and the other half picking up equipment while your spread truck partner drove. It took some precision driving skills and timing because the greatest danger in the field was vehicle 'interaction'. I would witness a number of accidents, often with stationary objects, due to inattention. To the amusement of all. Note to self: do not ever get complacent in the field!

By day three my arms and legs were covered in bruises. I ached all over from constant bending and cable-rolling, compounded by the full stack I took on day two. I was wrangling a tangled cable and got my foot caught and fell to the ground on top of a prickle bush with a thud, much to Owie's amusement.

'You look like Brer Rabbit in the Briar Patch', he hooted. His infectious laugh made me crack up too. Petey reached out a hand to help me up, always looking out for me in those early days, making sure I was drinking enough water and taking regular bathroom breaks. This wasn't always easy, since we would walk kilometres from our hard stand, where our equipment and the portable toilet was.

As I washed the dirt from my sore and sorry body that night in the shower, I noticed one dark spot that I couldn't seem to shift on my inner thigh. I gently ran my finger over the spot, which was raised up and not budging. I leant down for a closer inspection.

There was a fucking tick in my thigh and, to my horror, it was firmly embedded!

I told myself to stay calm as I got out of the shower, wrapped myself in a towel and picked up my phone to google 'How to remove a tick'. I snapped a quick photo of it so I could zoom in and get a good look.

Step 1: Use clean, fine-tipped tweezers to grasp the tick as close to the skin's surface as possible. I rummaged in my makeup bag for tweezers, grateful that I never left home without them (thanks to perimenopause and new hair growth on my face). Gotta love the aging process: the hair on my head was thinning and the hair on my face growing.

Step 2: Pull forward with steady, even pressure....

I turned the bedside lamp on and positioned myself on the seat next to the bed with my legs spread wide. WOW, what I must look like right now I thought. I tried to steady my hand so I could get a firm grip on its head. Three big deep breaths in and, with one swift movement, I released the tick in one piece, almost gagging at the site of it.

Step 3: Thoroughly clean the bite area and your hands with soap and water.

I put the tick in some tissues and wrapped it in a plastic bag, then cleaned the bite area, and my tweezers.

Step 4: Send the tick photo to your family members to prove after just a few days out bush you are already becoming a tough cookie.

I sent the photo to my kids along with the caption: *They call me Grills, Bizz Grills.*

That was my initiation into toughening up. I also learned to open cocky gates, climb through barbed wire fences, and perform pre-starts on the vehicle. Simple shit I had never before done. Why do we not teach all girls this stuff? The more I learned, the more empowered I became. When someone made a comment about my weakness, I remember saying:

'Don't confuse being soft with being weak. One of the greatest strengths is to stay soft in a world that will make you hard if you let it!'

I was pleasantly surprised that most of the crew not only accepted my spiritual, nature-loving hippie side, but embraced it. I loved spending all day walking in the outdoors and would stop to capture photos of trees or rocks that caught my eye. I would often return to camp at the end of the day to find some of the guys had brought me some spectacular pieces to add to my collection of rocks.

One of the greatest challenges was finding the courage to talk on the two-way radio. I felt like I was a big kid playing pretend and struggled to keep a straight face, so I avoided it at the start. I'd been told many times that I have a high-pitched, childlike voice, and worried what it would sound like over the two-way. The radios were often a source of amusement, especially when someone would accidentally key on and private conversations would be broadcast to everyone and their dog.

Speaking of dogs, we were at the washdown one afternoon, doing a weed and seed clean on our vehicles (a requirement every time we moved from one property to another so there was no transference of weeds) when a blonde lady, Karen, walked past with a tall red dog that looked extremely malnourished. She looked at me with big sad eyes.

'She was found abandoned on a property.'

'Oh, that's so sad, who would leave this beauty behind?' I said in disbelief.

'I volunteer at the pound, walking the dogs in the afternoons, I see a lot of sad stuff.'

'I will never understand some humans!'

I reached out a tentative hand to give the beautiful pooch a pat.

'I've only got two days to find her a home or she will be put to sleep!'

I barely slept that night. Every time I closed my eyes, all I could see was the big sad eyes of Big Red. I didn't have my own home, so I couldn't have a pet myself, and Miki already had a dog and a yard that wasn't fenced.

The next day I started reaching out to everyone I knew to see if anyone could give her a home, but no luck. Then my soul sister Doris offered to pay the adoption fee while we kept looking for a home for Red. The council allowed me to pay the adoption fee and keep her at the kennels until I finished the hitch, I just had to buy her food and take her for a walk in the afternoon, which Karen kindly offered to help with if I worked late and couldn't make it.

The next day I decided it was time to give Big Red a new name, Lakota, which means friend. She had also made a new friend when a puppy arrived at the pound. 'Well now

I'm screwed', I thought. 'I can't take one and not the other.' I picked her up and was covered in sloppy puppy kisses.

'I think I will call you Clementine.'

'Bel,' my work buddy Miles said, 'you can't save them all!'

'But I can try.'

I snapped a photo and sent it off to Doris with the caption: 'I need a home too.'

That amazing woman found a home for them both! Clementine was to be picked up by the animal rescue in Kingaroy and Lakota was going to Animal Welfare League in Brisbane. The only problem was that I had to get Lakota back to Brisbane. I would be returning in convoy with my work colleagues in a few days' time, and I seriously doubted taking a dog with us would be allowed.

That evening, as we sat around the BBQ area with a cold beer in hand, I approached Artie, another one of our supervisors, to explain my predicament. He confirmed that it was against policy. Then he asked how big the dog was.

'Huge.'

'Let me think about it.'

The next day Artie pulled me aside and gave me permission to sneak the dog home with me. He was pairing me up with

Kenny for the drive because he knew he would be up for the dog mission.

I will never forget Lakota's reaction when I picked her up that morning. She stood on her hind legs and hugged me, her big paws over my shoulder. Kenny captured the moment on camera.

We returned to camp with Lakota 'hidden' on the back of the ute, between the back window of the cab and a big plastic tub filled with equipment. Owie started laughing when he saw her beautiful face, peeking inquisitively around the tub. I gave a sshhh sign and we all met for a brief toolbox meeting before getting in our vehicles and starting the journey back to Brisbane.

We weren't far down the road when Beau, one of the front crew guys, overtook us and we heard the familiar static of the two-way radio.

'Who's driving VL16 cos there's a giant dog on the back of your vehicle!'

Oh dear, this is the end of my seismic career I thought, and Kenny and I laughed. 'What do I say?'

'I guess you just answer the question, I'll wear the dog situation.'

We heard the static of the two-way again, then someone singing: *'Who let the dogs out.'*

We pulled into Jondaryan for our rest and Lakota was bombarded with love from the entire crew.

I went home with a newfound strength and courage and enough money to support myself for the next two months on the road, and with a big red dog called Lakota.

An old man was walking on the beach one morning after a storm. In the distance, he could see someone moving like a dancer. As he came closer, he saw that it was a young woman picking up starfish and gently throwing them into the ocean.

'Young lady, why are you throwing starfish into the ocean?'

'The sun is up, and the tide is going out, and if I do not throw them in, they will die,' she said.

'But young lady, do you realise that there are many miles of beach and thousands of starfish? You cannot possibly make a difference.'

The young woman listened politely, then bent down, picked up another starfish and threw it into the sea.

'It made a difference for that one.'

Adapted from the original by Loren Eisley.

Working on a seismic crew

Rescuing Big red

CHAPTER SEVENTEEN

Belinda's Big Bus Tour

The kids had been working on the bus conversion while I was away, and it was looking great. The clock was ticking. We had only three weeks until my departure and a lot to get done in that time.

One week before I was to hit the road, we put the finishing touches on my now-purple beauty. Every part of that bus had been lovingly restored for the journey ahead. The exterior covered in brain injury awareness slogans symbolised the mission I was on. The interior was my inspiration. My original 80s record collection lined the roof, Bon Jovi memorabilia and family photos on the walls. My café dining table was a working space invader machine from the 80s with a perspex top; neon-yellow seat covers made the dining area pop. The pièce de résistance was the purple, fur-lined drivers bay, inspired by the film, *Get Him to the Greek*. If life slipped me any Jeffries on the road, I could '*stroke the furry wall*'.

I had been raising funds on a Go Fund Me page and had planned a fundraising night at the Stones Corner Hotel in Brisbane to launch the trip and, hopefully, to buy the fuel to get me around the country. I was still a long way from my goal.

I had a lot of support from Synapse, Australia's Brain Injury Organisation, in the lead-up to the trip. The CEO Jennifer (also a Bon Jovi fan), had connected me with their media and marketing wiz Ben Craig. Ben documented the weeks leading up to the trip on film and assisted me in contacting local media in some of the towns I was planning to travel through. He also organised some decal wraps for the bus, which was now ready to hit the road. 'Belinda's Big Bus Tour for Brain Injury Awareness' and 'Synapse' were now emblazoned across the front and sides of the bus, where 'Chasing Jon' used to be. It occurred to me that I was no longer chasing Jon but, inspired by his example, was now chasing my own purpose.

On Saturday 15th of July, 2017, my family and I boarded the lovingly renovated bus and headed to the Big Bus fundraiser at the historic Stones Corner Hotel. The proprietors had kindly offered us the venue free of charge for our fundraiser.

Buzz and the band were the main act for the evening, and my Miki, her good friend Jonathon, as well as my dear friend Lee and his partner Sam rounded out our support acts. Everyone was donating their time in support of the cause, and countless people turned up to give me an incredible send off on the journey of a lifetime.

On Tuesday July 18th, I set off from Brisbane on Belinda's Big Bus Tour for Brain Injury Awareness. I was on a mission. My big purple bus would be a moving billboard and a beacon of hope for brain injury survivors and their carers. I planned to drive from community to community around Australia delivering Synapse booklets and resources to rehabilitation centres and hospitals and meet with individuals and media in an attempt to break down barriers for those affected by brain injury.

I had only raised enough funds to get halfway, but with engagements booked on a tight schedule, including loved ones flying in and out of various airports to join me along the way so I always had a support person, any delay was out of the question.

I was shitting myself about driving this big bus such a long distance. I had only driven it a couple of times and, on top of that, I was concerned the old beauty may not make the distance. But I pushed those concerns aside and took a leap of faith, deciding that being on a mission for the greater good would bring good fortune on the road, just as it had on the maiden voyage to Broken Hill four years earlier.

Don't be afraid to take risks. Sometimes the biggest rewards come from the biggest leaps of faith – Jon Bon Jovi.

The first official stop on the tour was the Big Prawn in Ballina for a strategically placed photo of the bus. I wanted to get photos of the bus in front of as many iconic Aussie locations as possible to create awareness from community to community, especially in regional areas where resources are even more limited.

The second stop was the tiny township of Iluka in the Clarence Valley on the north coast of NSW. The drive in was breathtaking with the little country road hugging the ocean.

The small fishing village of Iluka, a local Aboriginal word meaning 'near the sea', has a population of around 1700 people.

Jeanette and Russ greeted me with the warmest welcome. They'd offered to park my bus in their driveway overnight and hook up to their electricity to save site fees at a caravan park. They had prepared chowder from freshly caught fish with hot bread rolls for dinner, a welcome surprise.

The bus didn't have running water or a working kitchen, but I had a toaster, kettle and little camping gas burner so I could cook basic meals like toasted sandwiches, noodles and soups, so freshly caught fish was a treat.

On day two the first destination was Grafton for a photo of the bus in front of the big bridge. My friends John and Dyna came from Grafton, also known as the jacaranda capital of Australia.

'Make sure you get your photo of the bus in front of the Grafton Bridge,' John said before my departure.

The little grey bridge was a lot smaller than the image John and Dyna had created in my mind. My sister-in-law Mandy was with me on this first leg of the journey and snapped a photo of the bus and me parked in front of the bridge. I uploaded it to my bus tour's official Facebook page with the caption: 'Hello Grafton.'

Grafton's *The Daily Examiner* had published an article before my arrival with the headline: 'Purple Bus to Bring Brain Injury Awareness to Grafton!'

This was the first official newspaper story on the tour, part of my idea to make the bus a moving billboard. It was proof that my intent to shine a light on brain injury survivors in regional communities was going to work.

Ten minutes down the road to Coffs Harbour from Grafton, I pulled over to take a call from John.

'That's the wrong bridge, you nutter. The Grafton Bridge is a lot bigger than that.'

'I did think it was a lot smaller than you described.' We cracked up laughing. Coffs was my first official stop. I delivered a box of Synapse booklets to the wonderful staff at the Mid North Coast Brain Injury Rehabilitation Centre, which supports brain injury survivors on the mid–north coast of NSW. The team there was excited to get a look at the big purple bus, and grateful for the resources we delivered to their clinic door.

I'd booked a site for the night at the Clog Barn Holiday Park, on the Pacific Highway in the centre of town. It's a family-run tourist attraction with a taste of Holland's charm. After checking in, we took a stroll around the miniature Dutch Village: replica Dutch buildings, beautifully manicured gardens, working windmills and garden railway.

We watched a clog-making demonstration: a block of wood placed into a machine and shaped into a clog. Once the outside was complete, the wood was removed from inside with multiple tools then neatened up with a blade. It was presented to me with the base still intact to proudly stand on a cupboard in my bus, a reminder of my visit to this unique tourist attraction.

Day three began with a bus-brewed coffee on my little gas burner, then a visit to the property's Big Omas Coffee House for some of their delectable Dutch pancakes and a cappuccino to fuel the day ahead.

Back at the bus we met with a local, Liz, whose son Jake had sustained a brain injury in 2010, aged twenty-four, after a coward-punch to the head. Jake was airlifted from Coffs Harbour Hospital to Royal North Shore Hospital in Sydney where he received lifesaving surgery.

Liz sat across from me in the bus and courageously shared her journey as a carer for her beautiful son. Jake will require physical and emotional care for the rest of his life. She told me how lucky I was that my son had been able to return to the level of independence he had and I was. We shared tears of understanding, knowing the pain and the cost brain injury had on our sons and families. One punch can steal the future and cause irreparable damage. A reporter from the local paper arrived to interview Liz and me: two mothers, now friends, united to create community awareness for brain injury survivors and their families, and fight for better resources.

I hit the road again, southbound. The next stop was Mid North Coast Brain Injury Rehabilitation Centre in Port Macquarie, and a lunch meet with a brain injury survivor. Then on to Bonny Hills, 20 km south of Port.

I pulled into Reflections Caravan Park for the night as the sun was setting. The view from our headland campsite overlooking Rainbow Beach as the sun descended took my breath away. When the park's owners saw the bus and slogans, they insisted I stay for free. After a quick tour of the inside, they declared it the best bus to ever visit.

I was increasingly concerned about a grinding sound when I turned the steering wheel, only days into a five-and-a-half-week journey.

As if he could sense it, I got a phone call from my old bus driving mate Bolly, wanting to know how the bus was running. When I described the sound to him, he guessed it was the power steering and asked if I wanted to make a short inland detour on my southbound drive to Sydney to visit him and my old seismic crew at Denman so he could look at the bus for me.

Denman is a small country town in the Upper Hunter Region surrounded by rolling vineyards and national parks. Half of the crew were staying at a motel in the town centre, the other half at Denman Van Village where, again, I was offered a campsite for free in support of my charity trip.

Late afternoon my old crew began one by one to roll into the park: Owie, Bolly, Farron, Petey and Kenny. They were all super excited to see the big purple bus I had talked so much about when we worked together in Chinchilla.

'You're doing it Bel, good on you mate!' Owie said proudly.

It was late in the day so we decided to first head to dinner at the Denman Hotel where the rest of the crew were staying. I felt like I was driving a school bus full of kids who laughed and joked for the short ride to the hotel. Conscious we had a mission back at the park, we didn't linger, but boy was it nice to see the team again, albeit briefly.

Back at the park, Bolly, Owie and Kenny set to work inspecting the bus. Farron, ever the prankster, appeared with a marker in hand threatening to add a letter T to the end of the Belinda's Big Bus's slogan before I shooed him away.

'Your power steering is leaking fluid,' Bolly informed me.

'I'm going to label the parts under the bonnet,' he said, 'and I want you to do a pre-start on the bus every day, just like you did when you were on hitch with us. I'm going to go with you to pick up some steering fluid tomorrow. Make sure you keep the oil topped up and it should be okay.'

There are genuinely good people in this world, who restore your faith in humanity. Bolly is one of them. We spent the rest of the evening playing on the space invader machine and sharing a laugh or two, the concerns that had been weighing on me alleviated. The following morning, I awoke to an icy cold bus, my little electrical blow heater barely heating any of the large open space lined with windows. It wasn't just the interior that was cold, the engine didn't want to start either.

'I'll show you a little bush mechanics,' said Farren. 'When the engine is cold, get someone to place a rubber thong over the exhaust as you turn the ignition over, and Bob's your uncle, she'll roar to life.'

Being the prankster, I didn't believe a word until he and Owie gave me a demo. The bus roared to life! I roared too, with laughter at the absurdity of what I had just witnessed.

Bolly joined me on the bus for a quick excursion to pick up some power steering fluid, then a demonstration of what I needed to check daily before I resumed my journey southbound to Sydney. I was sad to say goodbye to my old mates.

My vision of creating a wave of awareness was working. Newspapers all over the country were running stories on the big bus tour, but most impactful were the messages I was receiving on the facebook page from brain injury survivors and carers. People came out to meet me wherever I went so they could share their story with someone who understood.

Hi, I just saw you on the Pacific Highway and jumped straight on to share and will be making a donation next week for this fantastic cause. If you need anyone to share their stories of being affected by brain injury, I would be more than happy to help as I have been a carer from the age of seven as my single mother had a motorcycle accident in 1999 and suffered from a traumatic brain injury and it tremendously affected our family. Anything I can do to create awareness would be excellent, I could even put you in contact with my mother. Thank you for your fantastic work! ~ C

I was nervous as hell driving into Sydney in my big old bus, but excited to meet the Sydney Synapse team and Courtney's mum. She came out to meet me and trustingly shared her brain injury story with me. I was also excited that Miki and D flew in to join me on the next leg of the tour.

The miles clicked over and so did the towns, messages, and meetings...

Wishing you an extraordinary journey BBBT, may you change lives for the better through this wonderful project. ~ R

I wish you were heading further North in Queensland. My son suffers from NMDA Receptor Encephalitis, and I get his school to have an awareness day each year. ~B

My brother is in Adelaide at the moment having botox on his arm, he had a severe TBI last year and has significant right sided weakness amongst other things. Would love any info you have as since he moved from Sydney, he has very limited support/services. ~ J

Congratulations on your tour. It is wonderful to see. My accident happened in 1969 when I was 16 years old. There was no understanding of brain injury back then and over the years I have coped and now help people who are starting the long journey with a brain injury. Thank you so very much for your work. God Bless. ~A

Ben from Synapse had arranged for me to deliver some booklets to the Canberra Hospital Brain Injury Rehabilitation Unit. The lovely staff were waiting out front as I pulled in to deliver some boxes of books and beanies from the Bang on a Beanie campaign.

My next intended pitstop in Canberra was Parliament House. As I drove up Parliament Drive, circling Parliament House, I noticed an official-looking vehicle on my tail. Giggling, Miki suggested it was time to move on.

We continued the less official part of the tour, including the National Library where we took a break to explore the visiting exhibition and have a warm cuppa in the onsite café.

I have always loved Canberra, ever since I visited on a school excursion in grade six. The capital is surrounded by forests and close to the Australian alps, snowcapped mountains visible from the city in winter.

I woke to the coldest morning yet, a thin layer of ice covering the bus and a cold engine that didn't want to start.

'Don't worry, I know what to do.'

I asked D to get in the driver's seat and turn the engine over on my command. Miki followed me to the back of the bus and cracked up laughing, just like I had days earlier when I placed a rubber thong over the exhaust. I hope this works, I thought, or I'm going to look like a bloody dickhead!

'Okay, start her up!'

The bus roared to life, much to our amusement!

I was days away from running out of fuel money and had been trying not to worry when I received a call from Paul. A civil engineering company he worked with had generously offered to sponsor the remaining fuel for the tour. The relief was overwhelming; I would complete this tour, as I'd dreamed, thanks to the generosity and support of generous people.

We added the All Roads company logo, which they'd posted to Canberra, to the side of the bus before we crossed back into NSW.

We passed through Yass and Jugiong on the road to Gundagai, singing the famous song as we pulled in to get a snap of the bus in front of the iconic statue of the Dog on the Tuckerbox. Legend has it the statue was inspired by the 1850s poem 'Bullocky Bill' by Charlie 'Bowyang' Yorke.

Holbrook

Albury

Tocumwal

Echuca

Cohuna

Swan Hill

Town after town. We crossed the border from NSW to Victoria, message after message coming in with every mile we travelled.

Thank you for doing what you are doing. It means so so much.

On 7 Feb, 2016 I was involved in a motorbike crash that I only narrowly survived. As a result I had to relearn how to walk, talk and eat. 3 months in hospital and continual recovery since. In that time my wife has left, leaving me with our two young boys. Things haven't been easy, but I really feel for the people around me including my family. Thank you for raising awareness for the need of support for not only survivors but also their family members. I'm proud of what you are doing. Awesome job! ~ An

Hi Belinda, I would love to chat with you. I just saw your post about your son. Our story is similar however my son made a miraculous recovery (it seemed), although almost 6 years on we are still seeking a path forward. This period has been filled with good and bad and he is undiagnosed formally to this day as 'nothing shows up'. Would love to talk to you. Love to you. ~ J

My final stop in Victoria was the vibrant city of Mildura on the beautiful Murray River. For the first time since leaving Brisbane I wouldn't be sleeping in the bus. A cozy, warm bed awaited me at my dear friend Tambi's who had relocated from Broken Hill to Mildura a few years earlier. She insisted we stay with her and I was not going to refuse the opportunity to spend even a brief time with my dear friend. Tambi couldn't wait to check out the bus, very impressed with my 80s décor. I gave her a personal bus ride to her weekly game of basketball, then we went for dinner in town while Miki and D chilled out at her house.

It was a welcome respite to have a normal evening with a friend before I set off for Broken Hill the following day, eager to see family and friends. Jason had organised for Bel's Big Bus to attend Bells Milk Bar, an informal gathering and media opportunity with the local paper.

The gathering was a lovely mix of family, friends, local allied health professionals, brain injury survivors and media representatives. Jason generously donated $1 from every drink sold to the cause, another of those earth angels who bring light wherever they go.

I gifted myself a day off from the official tour to spend time with my loved ones, Bek, Supa, Al, Rach, Damo and Isabelle and the Arnolds; food for my soul before beginning the long journey to the Northern Territory.

I drove north on one of the longest stretches of road, surrounded by Australian desert. I was driven by adrenaline, but also, at times, strong emotion, reliving my own experience of Dylan's accident and recovery day after day.

I'd shared many moments of true connection with people who trusted me with their stories. Every story was unique, but the common theme was always lack of resources, lack of understanding and lack of awareness. All these factors were present from the moment of the brain injury throughout the rehabilitation journey, if lucky enough to receive rehabilitation.

There were many light moments on the tour also, most of which seemed to occur as I tried to position the bus in front of the BIG things all around the country. It had seemed like a great idea in theory but proved quite challenging in some locations. By the time I was in the home straight, well, let's just say I drove straight past the Big Pineapple!

The bus drove like a dream, though people were worried I would break down in some remote area. I brushed this off, saying I would cover the bus in white light every day. I don't think that lessened their fears.

When I pulled into the Kulgera Roadhouse, at the southern end of the Stuart Highway in the Northern Territory, I was surprised to see a bus identical to mine. Its owners, equally surprised, shared their story of being broken down and stranded for over a month waiting for a part. It was the first time I seriously considered the idea that a breakdown was more a probability than a possibility. After a refuel, the big purple bus drove across the Red Centre to the most magnificent BIG thing in Australia. I was about to fulfil a lifelong dream: seeing Uluru. I will never forget that moment, driving down the Lasseter Highway, when I caught my first glimpse of the magnificent rock. I made the final drive with tears rolling down my face. Uluru, I would come to understand, is not a place you see but a place you feel. It gifted me the healing my soul needed at this mid-journey point, and I'm not just talking about the bus journey.

My final pitstop in the Northern Territory was Tennant Creek, where I witnessed one of the most beautiful desert sunsets. I sat in my camp chair in full appreciation of the simplicity of living on the road.

Across state lines between the NT and Queensland, I picked up an extra passenger, Mitch, a hitchhiker who had rolled his car. He jumped on board in Tennant Creek at the servo.

I did have a moment of hesitation and remembered scenes from *Wolf Creek*, but he looked banged up. 'When I saw the charity bus,' he said, 'I knew there was a good heart on board.' Thankfully I live to tell the tale. Mitch disembarked in Mount Isa Airport and was straight on a flight back home to Sydney.

I continued across the Capricorn highway, pulling into Dingo Roadhouse, 148 km west of Rockhampton, to do a radio interview by phone. As I was talking, I dropped off mid-sentence, astonished when I saw a convoy of utes pulling into the roadhouse. It was none other than my seismic exploration crew. The amazement on their faces as they caught sight of Belinda's Big Bus mirrored my own. What are the odds in a country this size that in the middle of nowhere I would run into the team I had worked with to save the money for this very trip.

As soon as I got off the phone, I raced down the stairs to be met by hugs from the team. I joined them for a quick bite at the roadhouse before we all went our separate ways.

That night I received messages from Bolly and Owie excited to tell me that whilst they were eating dinner in the mess, they'd seen me on the news on the big screen.

'Onya Bel, you did great on the news!'

On Thursday the 18th of August, 2017, I made my final journey, driving back into Brisbane. I had driven 8,121 km, through six states and territories, in thirty-two days visiting rehabilitation centres, hospitals and schools. My campaign featured in newspapers and on radio stations and television news all around the country.

I had just one more pit stop to make, and it was the most important one of all. I ended my journey where it all began, at the Brain Injury Rehabilitation Unit at the PA Hospital.

I was greeted by Dylan who was at work at the time. To see him in his work uniform, walking me into the very rehabilitation unit where he was once a patient, was such an impactful moment that I am not sure there are words. As he led me down the hallway, he took such pride in the fact that he was now on the other side of those doors, with the access key to get in, not vice versa.

I received a warm greeting from the wonderful staff of BIRU, whose work is literally changing lives. Then Dylan and I went outside to pose for some photos with the bus for the hospital newsletter.

I left the hospital with my kids, mum, and partner at the time on board the bus, off to Southbank where people had been invited to meet me upon my return in front of the ABC building and the Wheel of Brisbane.

We'd been hoping the ABC would run a story, but that was pushed aside after another Pauline Hansen stunt in parliament. As I pulled up in front of the building, tired and emotionally spent, there was a lone figure sitting on a bench seat, waiting to greet me. It was my dad, waiting for his little girl to come home.

Build it and they will come. - Field of Dreams

Setting off on Belinda's Big Bus Tour

Dylan and I out front of the PA Hospital, my final stop on Belinda's Big Bus Tour
Photo credit: Metro South Health

Miki and D on Belinda's Big Bus Tour

CHAPTER EIGHTEEN

Dancing with the Darkness

I was restless. I thought after the bus tour I would move forward with my own life without a sole focus on brain injury. It quickly became clear a lot more work needed to be done.

It was also clear that I was in no position to help anyone. I was without work again and still living at Miki's with Huddo. I had been seeing someone on and off the preceding three years but had never been able to bring myself to fully commit to the relationship in the way he wanted. I had met him when I had suffered my post-traumatic breakdown.

I had been happily single for five years but had been drawn in by Wayman's (not his real name) strong values and affectionate nature. He was an old-fashioned gentleman who called me his lady. I had been asking the universe to help me meet a loving and passionate man and the universe had delivered. Although still scarred from my divorce it would take six months before I could even say I was in a relationship.

The first year flew by and Wayman wanted more of a commitment and suggested moving in together. We started looking for a home but the home he decided on only had enough rooms for his children. When I asked where Hudson was going to sleep, he suggested the bus, so I never moved in.

This was one of the first big red flags. My children and I were not seen as equals.

I did continue to see him despite the red flags, because I had fallen in love with Wayman. He had showered me in love and treated me with respect most of the time. We had a very intimate, passionate relationship, so I pushed my reservations aside and continued with our relationship, finally agreeing to move in with him two years later.

Living together would highlight our very different belief systems. The loving and affectionate man with old school values slowly revealed himself to be someone with anger and control issues who dictated what I should believe, what I should wear and who should be allowed in my life and HIS house based on his beliefs.

Everyone has the right to their own spirituality, and we can co-exist with others who think differently to us, but he did not believe this. It became clear to me that this man weaponised his beliefs to try and control every part of my life.

I had not listened to the little voice inside that knew this was not right for me. I had moved in and was not sure how I was going to wriggle my way back out. The relationship had put some distance between me and my family and friends. I'd try to spend time with them without Wayman there and felt split in two for a long time.

It was easy to ignore the red flags when things were good and there were a lot of good times. We shared a love of nature and camping; we could sit for hours around a fire talking and laughing. So, I would 'try harder' to make it work. I would hold my hand over his heart as he slept and wish him healing and wholeness from his own inner turmoil.

In 2017 the announcement was made that there would be a referendum to amend the Marriage Act to allow for marriage equality. Wayman fiercely opposed the amendment and flicked jam all over me in one of his fits of rage when I voted YES.

I needed time alone and space to think, independent of anyone else's advice, so I contacted Buzz and asked if I could return to my seismic job. He instantly agreed, and within weeks I was heading back out bush.

Wayman was not at all happy about me going to remote locations to work with a bunch of blokes.

When I turned up for my second seismic hitch, I was met with a warm welcome from old friends Owie, Wayno, Kenny, Petey, Beau and Bolly. They were especially interested in hearing how the bus trip went and congratulated me on the tour's success.

I got behind the wheel of the Toyota Landcruiser and hit the open road in convoy with my crew. Freedom. What a gift it was to be able to earn an income that also gave me time alone on the land. I settled into a new rhythm of working away balanced out by weeks at home. Despite my continued absence, or perhaps because of it, the situation at home seemed to be escalating.

We received some devastating news that our dear friend Desi had been diagnosed with terminal cancer. I hadn't known Desi long, but he had instantly gained a permanent place in my and Miki's heart. We bonded over our shared love of music. He and Buzz had taken Miki under their wing. They'd nurtured her through some performance anxiety to perform with them at my most recent fundraiser 'Bike Ride for Brain Injury'.

I was on a job at Wondoan when I received the news that Desi only had days to live. I desperately wanted to return home, but he was no longer receiving visitors. He spent his final days surrounded by family and those that were like family to him.

Wayman messaged me wanting to know if I was coming home early or not. A feeling in the pit of my gut told me that he was hiding something.

I tried to push the feeling away. As I walked through a field a beautiful falcon followed me for hours. If I moved it would too, landing in a tree or on a fence beside me. My walking companion was an environmentalist who remarked that she had never seen anything like it before.

'I think it's trying to tell me something,' I told her. I'm sure she thought I was batshit crazy.

Back at camp, that evening I researched the symbolism of falcons. One interpretation stood out to me: the falcon symbolises freedom and bravery; it encourages you to listen to your intuition and trust your gut instinct.

Everything in my gut said Wayman was keeping secrets from me so I decided to do some digging. I won't go into specifics, but my search confirmed that he was not being honest with me.

I felt gut punched! His concern about whether I was coming home or not for the weekend was not about him wanting to comfort me, he was trying to find out if I would ruin his weekend plans!

I thought of the falcon. It was time to be brave.

The hitch came to an end and our convoy headed back to Brisbane. I was barely keeping my emotions in check. Desi had passed while I was away, surrounded by his loving family, including Buzz. It was devastating. Someone so vibrant and full of life taken so suddenly. I felt like I was grieving for Buzz as well, knowing how much he was suffering this loss.

Miki picked me up from the workshop and, as we drove back to her place, I gave her a brief update. She extended an instant invitation to move back in with her, D and Huddo. I accepted the offer but needed to get past Desi's funeral first. I would move in the day before I went back out on my next seismic hitch. It was hard not to feel like a failure, again needing my kids' help.

The week passed in a blur. Miki and I attended Desi's funeral, a fitting send-off for a man who was loved by many who were still reeling from the loss.

I felt like I was living in a pressure cooker. My usual ability to walk on eggshells, and to let things slide, gave way. Instead, I gave him some sassy comebacks to comments that were contradictory to the man I now knew he was.

This did not go down well. His anger was building.

On my final day in his home. I went to his underwear drawer, opened his old phone, and photographed messages and photos that contradicted the man he purported to be.

I deleted all our messages wanting to clear any energetic connection to him. I returned the phone and went to pick Hudson up for a day surgery he had scheduled.

Hudson was supposed to be in early, but he kept getting pushed back. I felt for him, he's a big guy and had not eaten, as instructed. Unbeknownst to me he hadn't had anything to drink either. When the nurse came in to take his blood pressure, he started to see stars and I watched him fall forward out of the chair in the examination room as if in slow motion.

I tried to catch him, but he was too heavy and strong for me. I heard a loud thump as Huddo hit the floor face first.

Instantly triggered, I screamed for help. What if he too had a head injury?!

Nurses came rushing from everywhere and before I knew it, Hudson was in a hospital bed, I was in a wheelchair beside him, and Miki had been called as my emergency contact. I will never forget her face when she arrived, shaking her head from side to side.

'Well, well, well, look at you two. I need to snapchat this shit!' Hudson and I laughed as she pulled out her phone.

'I woke up and all I could hear was mum screaming,' said Hudson.

'Yeah, sorry about that. I panicked.'

Hudson had done no permanent damage, but they'd have to postpone his surgery because he was on concussion watch. So, we packed ourselves up and went to Miki's house.

I was beyond exhausted. I did not want to return to Wayman's house, but it was the last night I'd ever spend there, so I summoned all my strength. I pulled into the driveway one last time and quietly entered the house.

In no state to talk, I showered and slid into bed beside Wayman for the last time. I fell asleep in his embrace as silent tears escaped my eyes and sadness engulfed me.

I woke to the sound of Wayman in the kitchen getting ready to leave for work. I wasn't sure whether to pretend to still be sleeping but something in me needed to say goodbye. I wandered in as he was going out the back door. He turned and kissed me on the cheek and said goodbye.

'Goodbye,' I replied sadly.

I watched him drive away, then there was no time to waste. I messaged Kyla to say the coast was clear. She'd left her home on the Gold Coast early and was waiting nearby for my text. She arrived within minutes and helped me pack up my belongings.

I needed to do one more thing. I'd printed all the messages and photos from Wayman's phone at Miki's the afternoon before. I spread them out on his bed and placed a letter I had written in the centre. The letter said that it was clear he was not an honest man, that he did not respect women and he did not respect me. And if I stayed with him, I did not respect myself. I told him never to contact me again.

This is what it really came down to. He seemed to be dealing with a lot of inner conflict, pushing his beliefs on others whilst not living up to them himself. Beliefs that did not align with mine. I realised, for the first time in my life, that it wasn't my job to fix him or to fix anyone. It was enough to try to fix all my own broken pieces.

How could I ever grow with someone who didn't see me as an equal. He'd once told me women should not be in positions of power because once a month, when they have a period, they are unstable. I thought about all the periods

I must have had over the years whilst raising three kids. And battling the health system, caring for my son through his recovery from a severe brain injury, taking on a large corporation in an anti-discrimination case, working out bush in extreme heat in remote locations with no toilet, all whilst having a monthly period.

'It's time to go Belinda, because it turns out he was always in your way, man!'

John and Dyna arrived right on time with their furniture truck, and we loaded it up then put all the remaining items into my big purple bus. I drove out of the driveway for the final time without looking back!

Ever felt like you were drowning, your arms flailing in the air and people walking by think you're waving at them, so they wave back with a smile? That's how I felt. No one could see how truly broken I was or understand why I was not my usual happy, positive self. I'm 'the strong one who has overcome so much'.

'It's not like you to be angry,' friends would say.

'Maybe I should've been angry a long time ago. If I had been, maybe I wouldn't have put up with some of the shit I've taken in my life.'

The person I was most angry with was myself, for allowing, for settling for being a doormat. I'd had this notion that being spiritual is all about the light, but I don't believe that's true now. Life is always going to be a balance of darkness and light, and if we don't face the darkness within ourselves and be authentic about it, then how are we supposed to heal?

The emotion at the end of a relationship in some ways feels like a minor death. We grieve for the future we thought we had. A little part of us dies when our hearts get broken. I had my trust broken by this man, and now I no longer trusted myself. How could I have been so wrong and so blind.

I put up with shit throughout my life because I never wanted to make a fuss. I'd been abused by men before but always tried to keep the peace. I needed to be angry! It was long overdue.

I went back out to work in the bush, but after a few days we were sent home due to rain. I was relieved. I wasn't in a good headspace and being away from my kids compounded my feelings of loneliness. Buzz put me in the workshop, so I still had an income. He, Denise and Deb were beacons of light, otherwise I was lost.

I needed to not feel. I went into the city with friends and drank copious amounts of alcohol, wandering off alone as I've been known to do when intoxicated.

I stood on a bridge looking down at the water, tears streaming. I was feeling grief and anger. I also felt like a burden, having to move back in with my daughter and her husband again. I was middle-aged and starting all over, for the third time! I'd given what little furniture I had away when I moved in with Wayman (who, I should add, had moved on to another relationship within weeks).

My soul was tired, my tears flowed and seemed to become one with the river below. I had a fleeting moment of feeling so tired and desperate that I understood how people take that step, where it's all over. We have a saying about it not being too weak to speak but what's the point if no one is listening!

A voice behind me brought me out of my trance, 'You look like you could use a friend.'

It was a young man wearing a long floral dress with sneakers and makeup.

'I could use a friend, too; this is the first time I've had the courage to dress this way.'

They reached out a hand to me and I took it like the lifeline it was. Off we walked arm in arm into Fortitude Valley, two strangers sharing our pain with one another.

After that night, I made the decision to take some time to feel the grief without trying to disconnect by drinking alcohol, hooking up with men, or the other quick fixes that prolong the healing process.

The first step was to look within at my own darkness.

I distanced myself from everyone and found companionship and solace in the only place that had always been there for me: my writing. I have always been able to write what I can't say.

The heaviness I feel inside, is like a weight I try to hide.

Behind a smile, a laugh, a grin.

Fighting a battle, I can't win.

The darkness closes in on me, I struggle just to breathe.

Can I fight another day?

It would be easier to leave.

Dancing with the darkness, I just can't see the light.

Faces flash before my eyes, I know I have to fight.

The love I feel must override, the crippling pain I feel inside.

The endless tears that I have cried.

I've got to win this fight, between the darkness and the light.

Chapter Nineteen

Buckleys

It was time to go back out into the field, but I didn't feel ready, so I took a job at a factory making canopies for four-wheel drives. I was in the window prep section installing locks and making sure the windows were ready for installation. It was summer and it was fucking hot inside the factory.

The humdrum of factory life gave me routine, but my soul still yearned to pursue a career in the creative arts. I thought about my journey writing 'Chasing Jon' and realised I lacked the experience to bring a big project from script to screen. I thought about my inspiration, Mr JBJ himself, and how he'd got his start playing gigs at small venues whilst sweeping floors at his cousin's music studio, the Power Station.

I needed to start at the bottom and learn everything I could about filmmaking, so I started putting feelers out for a job working as a production runner. Production runners provide assistance to the producers and coordinators, running around picking up whatever items are needed for the different departments and, most importantly, travelling the film rushes at the end of the day to the editors.

I was sending my resume out to various productions with no response when, out of the blue, I had a phone call from Jason, my filmmaker friend in Broken Hill. A feature film was soon to begin filming in my hometown.

Jason said they were looking for crew and offered to put my name forward for a position, but I would have to relocate to Broken Hill for two months. Dylan had recently met the girl of his dreams, his Pepper Potts he affectionately called her, and they were pregnant with their first child. A miracle given his journey, so taking this job would mean missing the birth of my first grandchild. This was a huge milestone for Dylan and one that just a few years earlier I thought he may never reach. Dylan and Chrissy had invited me to be present at the birth and I could think of no greater honour than to witness the moment my boy became a father for the first time.

I tried to put all thoughts of working in film out of my head and make the most of my new job, but I felt like a robot working on the assembly line. The sweltering summer was compounded by the heat inside the factory from the large oven where car parts would dry after being painted.

The noise made by various tools and by speakers blasting music from work cells made my head pound. This was about as far as one could get from working all day in nature.

The more jobs I tried, the more I realised that every career has its challenges, but at least some rewarded you financially for your labour. The factory job paid a minimum wage, and I wondered how those with families to support managed on such a meagre income. How would I be able to afford to move out into my own home with no partner or secondary income?

The buzzer signifying the end of the workday brought me back to the present. I laid down my tools and lined up with my co-workers to punch out at the machine. I was off to meet Dylan and Chrissy for an afternoon coffee date.

As I entered the coffee shop, the parents-to-be were enjoying a moment of laughter together. With only seven weeks to go until the due date, Chrissy had definitely popped since the last time I'd seen her.

I joined them at the table, and Dylan was unable to contain his excitement. 'We have decided on a name for our daughter!'

'Ooh, am I allowed to know what it is?'

'Aliana Belinda, we want to name her after both you and Chrissy's mum, whose nickname is Belinda.'

'I am honoured beyond words,' I said.

'Have you decided what you want to be called yet?' Chrissy asked.

'I've decided I want to be called Nanny B. I know some people have said I'm too young to be called nanna, but I love it, it's a title I'll be proud of!'

'Nanny B, I love it!' Dylan said.

'How is the factory going?' Chrissy asked.

'Like Groundhog Day.'

'Do you think you will stay there or look for something else?'

'Funny you should ask. I was just offered the opportunity to be put forward to work on a movie starring Bill Nighy! It would be a dream come true, but it's being shot in Broken Hill, so I said no. There is no way I'm going to miss being there to see Miss Aliana Belinda come into this world. The factory may not be my dream job but at least it allows me to stay home.'

I excused myself to go to the ladies. When I got back, Dylan said he had something he wanted to say, and insisted I hear him out before saying anything.

'Mum, you have been there for me my whole life, especially after my accident. You put your own life on hold to make sure I recovered, and I wouldn't be where I am today without you. Now it's your turn. I want you to go for the film job, it's the opportunity you have been working for and deserve to have! You will be an important part of Aliana's life whether you are there for her birth or not.'

I was dumbfounded. I mean yes, I wanted to take the opportunity, but missing the birth was not something I had even considered. If I got the job I wouldn't see or hold my granddaughter until she was a few weeks old.

'But I really want to be there, it's not a moment I will ever get back.'

'There will be a million moments you will be there for, and a million moments you won't, and that's okay,' Chrissy said. 'You can have both. I plan to.'

Chrissy had kept working through her pregnancy and planned to return to work six months after giving birth, because she needed to, but also because she enjoyed her job and the people she worked with. I thought about these generational shifts and realised that perhaps I had something to learn. As I crawled into bed that night, I thought about what Dylan and Chrissy had said. It was true, Aliana wouldn't remember if I was there at her birth or not, and what if being there meant missing the opportunity for the career I had dreamed of for so long. Another opportunity like it may never present itself again.

Maybe this was a test for me: to realise that it's okay to make myself a priority and, as a mum, to let go just a little more.

I decided I would contact Jason the following day to see if it was too late to put me forward. I closed my eyes and felt a glimmer of hope that my factory days may soon be over and my dream job finally within reach.

A week passed and, in one week, everything changed.

I arrived at my mother's house for a Mother's Day roast lunch, looking forward to spending the day with my family. It would be the last family meal I shared with them for a few months because the following day I would be on a flight to Broken Hill to begin work as a production runner on *Buckley's Chance*!

I'd interviewed for the position over the phone with Sandy Stevens, the film's production manager, just three days earlier. She'd offered me the position with a start date the following Tuesday morning.

As I entered the house I was met with the familiar aroma of a roast cooking and the sound of laughter. I saw mum in the kitchen, as usual a hive of activity. My kids and my cousin Ben were sprawled out around the small living area.

Noting Chrissy's absence, I asked Dylan. He said she was feeling a little unwell and had some pain in her back so had gone to her mother, Tina's, house. I assured him I'd drop by to see Chrissy before I left the following evening.

The kids all gathered at the table as mum and I began to serve up lunch. I felt like I should be cooking for her, it being Mother's Day, but she loved hosting these lunches and, since I still didn't have a home of my own, I didn't argue with her.

I could barely contain my excitement as I shared the few details I knew about *Buckley's Chance*. It was an Australian/Canadian co-production, a feature starring Bill Nighy and one of my favourite Aussie actors Martin Sacks.

Miki was super excited and jealous that I would get to work with Bill, who she was a huge fan of. The Canadian connection felt like a good sign, given the deep love and affection I have for the country. The only dark cloud was the knowledge that I wouldn't be present at little Aliana's birth. Still, I felt I had made the right decision to go. It had not been an easy one.

We fell into our usual family banter over lunch. Dylan received a phone call and excused himself from the table, returning moments later practically bouncing off the walls. Tina had taken Chrissy to the hospital: she was in labour, six weeks early!

Dylan and I raced out the door, promising to update everyone when we knew more.

We arrived at the hospital half an hour later, Dylan running until we found the maternity ward and located Chrissy's room. He asked a million questions and Tina updated us: baby Aliana's arrival was imminent.

'Looks like you are not going to miss her birth after all,' Chrissy said with a heartfelt smile, instantly replaced with a grimace as another contraction began.

'Are you okay darling?' Dylan asked, kneeling beside the bed. Chrissy responded with the rise of an eyebrow, saying everything she needed to without words. The contraction subsided and we could hear the rhythm of the baby's heart on the monitor. Tina was sashaying across the room towards me in time with the beat, which made me giggle.

'How exciting is this Nanny B.'

'Exciting beyond words Nanny T.'

I noticed the look on Dylan and Chrissy's faces.

'You're gonna have two mad nannas kid.'

They weren't wrong!

A nurse entered and informed us only two people were allowed in the room. Seeing my look of disappointment Tina offered to go out, but I wouldn't hear a word of it. Chrissy needed her mum and Dylan's support. I gave them both a quick squeeze and wished them the best and headed out to the waiting room.

I took a seat feeling a million emotions, including bewilderment that this was happening. I sent a quick update to the family and Miki replied saying she was going to head up to the hospital to wait with me.

Hours passed. My mind wandered back to a time, not so long ago, when I sat in a hospital waiting room wondering if my son was going to live or die. And now, seven years later, my boy was about to get a miracle of his own. I was pulled back to the present when Tina came running into the room.

'Come on Nanny B, you are not missing this moment, she's coming!' She grabbed me by the arm and pulled me into Chrissy's room where we stood quietly arm in arm as we watched with wonderment as little Aliana Belinda entered this world.

We were both in tears as we witnessed the moment both our kids became parents for the first time. We all breathed a sigh of relief when we heard Aliana cry. In an instant she was wrapped up by the medical team and, due to her prematurity, whisked away to be assessed. 'Go with her,' Chrissy instructed Dylan.

'I don't want to leave you,' he replied, looking torn in two.

'I will stay with Chrissy; you and your mum go with Aliana,' Tina said. We raced out of the room and headed to the Neonatal Intensive Care Unit. Dylan, the anxious new dad, stood protectively by his daughter's side as she was poked and prodded with needles and tubes.

I found it difficult to watch. It was a rough entry to this world for such a tiny little human, but I marvelled at modern medicine and the incredible work our health care workers do every day to save the lives of those we love.

Despite being six weeks premature, it seemed Aliana was a strong little lady. Her proud parents got one longed-for cuddle before she was placed in a humidicrib under lights where she would remain until her little body grew stronger.

I didn't get the opportunity to hold her myself but that didn't matter; she was going to be okay, and I had been blessed to be present at one of the most impactful moments in my son's life. Witnessing his calm strength and devoted love towards his new little family I felt at peace. My position in his life had now shifted to somewhere more on the periphery and it was indeed time to let go just a little more.

Nanna Rap

To my Ali B, from your nanny B,

You're the next branch on our family tree

And already loved so enormously

I already feel a love so deep

To see your dad's dream complete makes me weep

Tears of joy and of gratitude

And if you're anything like your nanny

You might have a bit of an attitude

Never dull your shine or your spark

They will light up your path when times are dark

And if there's any wisdom I can impart

On thee, it would be, society will try to tell you who to be

But you're already perfect, imperfectly

You don't need to buy products

To make you pretty or witty

True beauty's in your soul and shines through your eyes

Don't listen to the lies, society cries

That to be loved you need the perfect body and thighs

Cos someday you realise

Seeking external validation leads to a soul that dies

You're here for connection

Not a corporation's idea of external perfection

Always do you, the world will adjust

It needs your uniqueness, your freakness, your guts

Don't try to hide, the voice inside

Speak up, be brave, be strong and be bold

It's YOUR story that needs to unfold

Don't feel caged as you age

Each day's a new page, waiting to be be told

Take chances, travel, roam and explore

Open your heart to adventure and to love but of this you can be sure

Someday your heart will break

And you will want to numb the ache, that's a mistake

Healing takes feeling, even though you'll be reeling

You'll work your way through to start anew

Don't ever let pain harden you

Being alone does not mean incomplete

And being vulnerable isn't weak

From a loving heart, kind words you will speak

You never know how deep that can reach & impact the world

You are THAT special my girl

Gotta resist the urge to wrap you in cotton wool

Have to let you stumble and fall

It's how we learn to stand tall, it builds our resilience

Gives us strength to fight resistance

And the endurance we need to travel the distance

Through it all, I'll be by your side

On this journey called life I'll be your nanna with pride

I may not be able to give you many things

But you'll soon see, the best things in life are free

Like climbing a tree or sitting by the ocean, breathing

in the air

Lying under a star-filled sky without a care

Just know I will always be there

You'll always have my time, that's why I'm writing this rhyme

Even though some will think it's a crime, this old nanny writing a rap,

Pfft I don't care about that.

Love you with all my heart Ali B, I'm gunna be the best nanny I can be.

Dylan with Aliana

CHAPTER TWENTY

Banging The Drum

I stepped onto the tarmac in Broken Hill in a whirlwind of emotion. I was super excited to be home and to start my new job, but I was concerned for little Aliana, still in the humidicrib.

I picked up my hire car and drove straight to the production office in The Old Brewery on the northside of town.

The heritage building was a little slice of local history, the most popular of five breweries that, at the turn of the century, supplied beer not just to the local community but to most of the West Darling pubs right up to the Queensland border.

I parked the car thinking that my past and future had just merged into one. I had dreamed about working in film and television as a kid growing up in Broken Hill but thought the isolation of the town and its remoteness meant limited opportunities. How ironic that my first big opportunity was in the place I'd left in order to achieve this very thing.

I entered the old building. A few fold-out desks and office chairs were set up as a sparse, makeshift office. I cast my eyes around the room, a little nervously, looking for someone that seemed to be in charge. A graceful young woman crossed the room towards me, smiling. I accepted her outstretched hand.

'You must be Belinda, our production runner. I'm Tahlia, the Production Co-Ordinator, welcome to the team.'

'Thank you, I am really excited to be here!'

I was given a brief tour of the building where I was introduced to crew from various departments, and finally met Sandy, the Production Manager who'd telephone-interviewed me. Sandy welcomed me with an upbeat handshake and genuine warmth. It immediately calmed my nerves.

I was completely green, as they say, and I couldn't silence the little nagging voice in the back of my head, wondering if my brain was ready for this after years of labouring. But there was only one way to find out if I was able to again retain information.

I spent the day familiarising myself with the role and getting set up with a petty cash float. Before I knew it, I'd done my first day in the production office.

I packed up my computer and headed off to my cousin Bek's house. She had kindly offered me a room for the next six weeks. We were both looking forward to spending some quality time together. When I arrived, Bek gave me my own coffee mug, which matched hers. It felt like we were sisters, living together for the first time after some challenging years, post-divorce, for us both. There was so much time to catch up on.

My first week seemed to fly by. One of my tasks was gathering information for a welcome booklet, part of a pack, which I also helped put together, to be given to cast and crew when they arrived. I was also picking up items for the office and getting quotes.

I was probably a bit of a pain in the arse to my coordinator and production manager – I asked a lot of questions in my desire to do well. On one occasion Sandy asked me to get a quote for the hire of a scissor lift for the lighting department. Later that day, when I gave her the quote from the local hire company she stifled a giggle. 'B, what size is the scissor lift? $165 a day with a delivery fee of $27.50 doesn't sound quite right.'

'I didn't know they came in different sizes.'

Sandy patiently explained the purpose for the hire, and I resumed my mission armed with these details. Sandy's initial reaction to my first quote was explained by the forthcoming quotes, which were in the thousands.

Despite my naivety, Sandy never made me feel stupid. She encouraged me to ask questions if there was anything on which I needed clarification.

The following week, Greg, a legendary runner from the Gold Coast, arrived in Broken Hill as the film's second runner, though should I say first, given his wealth of experience! Greg was easy-going and shared his knowledge and lots of tips with me, both on the industry and our role in production. I learned a lot from him in a short space of time.

Sarah from Adelaide joined us as our production secretary, representing South Australia, which was nice since our team, that now also included travel coordinator Ryan, was predominantly from Queensland.

Lauren and Karleen, from the art department, were also from Queensland. They were very welcoming and warm and had a wicked sense of humour. I hit it off with them instantly. The Art Department has always been an area of interest for me. The entire team on this job were a great crew, and new friendships would continue when I returned to Queensland.

We had some locals joining us on crew, the first being Jason, of course, who had recommended me. He was working in the locations department, but also assisting with extras casting – filming the locals' auditions.

With Greg now on deck, I was leant to Jason one afternoon to assist with the locals' auditions. He had decided his Milk Bar was the perfect place to set up, so I met him at Bells, excited to learn about another aspect of filmmaking (and to check out the local talent of course).

It was my job to greet people as they arrived, getting them to fill out the required paperwork while Jason was filming. There were some familiar faces and also a lot of new ones.

The final audition was a guy called Billy whom I'd never met before. We fell into easy conversation and were chatting like old friends by the time Jason called him in for his audition. I really had been checking out the local talent!

I tidied up my paperwork and before I knew it Billy's audition was done, and it was time to do mine. Yes mine!

I had let Jason convince me to audition for the role of the waitress. I was nervous as hell, more so because I knew him so well.

'I don't think I can do this.'

'Give it a shot, what have you got to lose.'

'Well, my dignity for starters.'

I took my place waiting for Jason's cue. 'Action' he called out. I sauntered over to the diner booth where he was sitting with camera in hand, pretending to be my customer. Attempting to avoid eye contact, I chewed gum and gave my best surly waitress impression.

'What can I get ya?' I muttered.

'How's the meat pie?' Jason asked off camera.

'Well, let me tell ya, if it was between me and the meat pie, me husband chose the meat pie.' Dammit, I lost it at the end.

'Sorry, I stuffed that up, and I think I rolled my eyes.'

I was giggling and so was Jason. He called 'reset' and I went back to my starting position to await his cue.

Multiple takes later we called it a day. After watching my own performance, I knew I was also calling it a day on my acting career. I cringed at the thought of who was going to see this award-winning performance of mine. We usually had Sundays off, but that Friday afternoon, as I was packing up my desk, Sandy asked me if I would be interested in working half a day on Sunday driving the producer and his wife to pick up some groceries.

The extra money was welcome, and I was loving meeting the many personalities a film crew attracts. Our producer, Gilbert Adler, who I'd seen around the office a couple of times, was an interesting character. Born in New York and a writer/producer/director, he had a career that spanned three decades, including *Tales from the Crypt*, *Charmed*, *Superman Returns*, *Valkyrie* and *Constantine*. His wife Jeannie was a writer also.

On Sunday morning I knocked tentatively on the door to Gil and Jeannie's apartment. I was greeted by the most angelic woman, who seemed genuinely happy to meet me. So did Gil. They introduced themselves and followed me to the car.

'Are you a local Belinda?' Jeannie asked as we drove to the supermarket.

'I'm Broken Hill born and bred but moved to Queensland when I was twenty.'

'How marvellous,' Jeannie said. 'We love it out here. The landscapes are simply breathtaking.'

After a couple of hours running errands, Gil asked if I would like to join them for a coffee at the Silly Goat. I agreed, eager to hear more about their life back in Vancouver, which they now called home. Vancouver just happens to be one of my favourite places on the planet.

We took our seats after Gil placed our order. They were just as eager to hear about me.

'What made you get into the creative arts Belinda?' Jeannie asked.

I gave them a brief rundown on my later journey into the arts after starting a family early in life and my strong belief that film and TV are a powerful tool to reach people and have an impact.

I shared my passion for rehabilitation and, as a brain injury advocate and ambassador for the Hopkins Centre, how I had been researching the healing benefits the arts can have.

'I would love to help,' said Gil. 'We could offer a day on set and a "meet and greet" with Bill Nighy as a prize. You could raffle it off to raise funds.'

I sure wasn't expecting that. My mind was turning over at a million miles an hour. The prize would have to be local, and I was only here for six weeks. What on earth could I organise and pull off in such a short space of time? Maybe it was time to take another lesson from the Book of Jovi.

Projects are made possible by partnerships; it's called the power of we.~ JBJ

'That is an amazing offer and I gratefully accept. Thank you!'

Jeannie's face lit up. 'Oh Belinda, this is just fabulous, what will you do?'

'I have an idea but will have to work on the finer details and come back to you both during the week.' We wrapped up our coffee date and I drove them back to their accommodation, my mind in another world. What the feck was I going to do with this prize?

Back at Bek's house late in the afternoon, after running my own errands, I was greeted by the sweet aroma of cakes and pastries. Like Grandma Addie and Aunty Maria, Bek was an amazing cook who took great joy and pride in creating amazing dishes. My last-minute purchase of a bottle of Tennessee honey whiskey was the perfect accompaniment, on the rocks, for a late afternoon tipple. This turned into an 80s music dance party in our unicorn and llama pajamas, respectively.

I put all thoughts of a fundraiser out of my mind so I could be present in this rare moment with my cousin. Bizzy

Bee and Becky Boo were the inseparable duo through our childhood and teen years, and we reminisced about a time long ago when life seemed so much easier, sneaking out our bedroom windows to hang out, dancing the night away at the Blue Light Disco with our big hair and fingerless gloves, and all the boys we had loved *real bad*.

My trip down memory lane was interrupted when I received a message from Billy asking me out to dinner. We had exchanged a couple of messages after meeting at his audition, but I was surprised by his invitation to go on an actual date!

'Hellooo, Bizzybee.'

Bek waved a hand in front of my face to get my attention. I told her what the text message was about.

'Isn't that called the casting couch?' Bek laughed.

'NO! I wasn't the one doing the casting and technically, I was also auditioning,' I said indignantly.

'You've been in town one week and already you're going out on a date,' she laughed.

'I haven't said yes yet, and I'm not sure I will, I don't know how old he is, but he is definitely younger than me.'

'How young?'

'I really don't know but I would guess around 35.'

'What's his name? Maybe I know the family.'

I passed on all that I knew about Billy, which wasn't much, but she didn't know him.

'He knows I'm in town with the film for a short time so he clearly isn't interested in anything serious so maybe I will go. It will be a big step forward for me to go out with a guy who actually knows my name at this point but without any pressure.'

So, I replied to Billy with an 'I would love to' just as Salt and Pepper's 'Push It' came on the playlist. We jumped straight into the famous dance moves, singing at the top of our lungs 'pu pu push it real good!'

Motivated by the bus tour and the number of people who'd reached out to express their desperate need for resources and rehabilitation, I'd begun researching arts-based rehabilitation therapies. The two that had my interest were dance and music-based therapies, which I believed could be adapted to benefit the brain injury community and their carers.

I'd begun researching dance in Brisbane, but the option that seemed a good fit for Broken Hill was drumming. 'Djembe drumming' has been proven to stimulate cognitive function, reduce stress and improve coordination.

Suddenly a lightbulb came on. If I could find a local facilitator, we could raise the funds to purchase some djembe drums and donate them to the local brain injury rehabilitation service, then fund the facilitator and their occupational therapist to trial a drumming class for people affected by brain injury.

I had six weeks to pull this off and was already working a six-day week but I like a challenge. I decided to give it everything I had. In the words of JBJ, I could 'sleep when I'm dead'.

I was dizzy with excitement. I picked up my phone and put out a call on Facebook to the Broken Hill community, asking if anyone knew of any local djembe drummers. The notifications started pinging and, by the end of the day, I had a number of messages directing me to two women who ran a weekly drumming group in the offices behind the Broken Hill Base Hospital.

A few phone calls later and I had a meeting organised for Sunday at Gloria Jeans with the drummers, Ali and Nicky, as well as the therapists from Interhealth, to discuss putting this ambitious plan into action.

I emailed Gil and Jeannie to let them know the wheels were turning on the why, now I had to start planning the where and how I was going to hold the fundraiser! A soft rat a tat tat on my bedroom door interrupted my thoughts.

'Shouldn't you be getting ready for your date?' Bek said with an eyebrow raised.

'Shit! I lost track of time!' I said, just as my phone began to ring. It was Miki.

'Hey toots, is everything okay?'

'Yeah, was just calling to say hi, is everything okay with you? You sound weird,' she laughed.

'Yes yes, all good here, can I call you tomorrow night for a catch up? I'm just heading out.'

'Where are you going on a school night?'

'Geez who's the parent here? If you must know I'm going out on a date....'

'With whom?' she demanded.

'His name is Billy, no one you know, toots. Look, sorry, but I've got to run, I'll talk to you tomorrow night. Love ya!'

I hung up and raced off to the shower.

Half an hour later, Billy arrived to pick me up right on time. I hadn't been out on a date since my last relationship ended so I felt slightly nervous, but as we climbed into the car, the space filled with his earthy scent and his warm smile immediately put me at ease.

At the Astra, we were seated at a table towards the back of the restaurant and offered a drinks menu. We ordered wine and fell into an easy rapport. I remembered why I'd said yes to this date: there was no pressure from this guy, so I didn't need to put any on myself.

He told me about his work at the mines and his passion for education and knowledge. But his eyes burnt with fierce pride when he spoke of his love for his family and for the country. He was telling me a story about one of his older brothers, but I could only hear my own thoughts: *Older brother? My little bit of local research had me thinking he was the eldest.*

'How old is your brother? I asked casually.

'He just turned 30.'

I almost spat my wine across the table.

'If you don't mind me asking, how old are you?'

I was almost afraid to hear the answer.

'Twenty-eight,' he said.

'Twenty-eight!!' My voice sounded several octaves higher.

'Age is just a number!'

'Well, your number is a little too close to my eldest son's number. How old do you think I am?'

'Late thirties maybe.'

'I'm forty-five, I probably went to school with your mum!'

I glanced around the restaurant to make sure no one I knew was there. This would be great content for the gossip mill tomorrow!

As I arrived home, I noticed some missed calls from Miki and, concerned something was wrong, I called her back despite the hour. She answered with an accusatory tone.

'You! Are! A! Cougar! He is the same age as my husband!'

I laughed.

'Actually toots, he's a year older than your husband and cougars go out looking for younger men, I had no idea what his age was until tonight. So how on earth do you know?'

'I stalked his Facebook.'

'Geez girl, have you got nothing better to do? I'm too tired for this, I'll call you tomorrow. Love you.' It's interesting how we seem to look at an older woman dating a younger man through a completely different lens than an older man dating a younger woman, which seems widely accepted.

We would become firm friends, and still are. I've had some of my deepest conversations with Billy, who has wisdom beyond his years, and always treated me with respect and kindness. He also taught me a lot and helped me heal in more ways than he could ever know. What a free feeling it was to connect with someone who is completely honest and had zero expectations.

The week was a whirlwind! The drumming meeting was a huge success with all parties excited to participate in running a pilot program. I'd pulled together a fundraiser to be held at the Outback Resort, where we would sell raffle tickets for the day on set, kindly donated by Gil and Jeannie. The then local paper, *The Barrier Daily Truth*, was running a story on the film shoot, and Gil insisted they include a story on me and the fundraiser in the same issue.

The headline 'It's Bill Nighy, Actually' was accompanied by a photo of Bill and fellow actor Milan Burch. The caption underneath read: 'YOUR CHANCE TO JOIN TOP FILM CREW: Page 3.'

I turned the page and there I was with the headline 'Better than Buckley's'....

One lucky local will have the chance to spend a day on a film set thanks to a fundraiser for brain injury awareness.

As the movie 'Buckley's Chance' is currently being shot in Broken Hill, a former local working on the set had the chance to raise funds and awareness about brain injury.

Production runner Belinda Adams shared her journey of her son Dylan's near fatal accident and traumatic brain injury and rehabilitation with the film's producer Gil Adler.

Speaking with Mr Adler and his wife Jeannie, Ms Adams had no idea where it would lead. 'Hearing how Belinda cared for her son through years of rehabilitation after traumatic brain injury (tbi) to be living an independent life again inspired me to want to give back to the local community,' Mr Adler said.

The article covered my bus tour and dedication to brain injury rehabilitation, and the importance of resilience, as well as the quickly formed partnership between myself, Nicky Wright, Social Work Academic at Broken Hill University of Rural Health, and local facilitator of the DRUMBEAT program, social worker and African drummer Ali Lloyd. Details were provided of how, where and when people could support the fundraiser. It was a dream-like moment to be in the paper with legendary actor Bill Nighy.

The turnout at the fundraiser was impressive, especially given the very short time we had to plan and execute the event. It was overwhelming to see so many of my fellow crew and cast members, and the local community, all coming together to generously support the initiative.

We raised $2000 that day but still needed another $3000 to reach our goal. Nicky's husband, Lindsay, who I had recommended to Sandy for the position of personal assistant to Bill, organised for us to attend his club's weekly trivia night.

I was feeling completely burnt out and, due to exhaustion, unable to speak. 'I just can't do it tonight,' I said tearfully. 'Then we will do it for you,' Lauren said. Then she, Lindsay and Denise, the film's accountant, picked up the donation buckets to sell tickets for me. The night's ticket sales, along with a generous $500 donation from my good mate Jason, bumped our fundraising total up to $3500. A Go Fund me page pushed the tally to $4000 over the next couple of weeks, but we were still $1000 shy of the target with only a week until we wrapped principal photography.

One night I pulled into Umberumberka Reservoir, our filming location for the night, to be greeted by Lindsay, envelope in hand. 'I have something for you from Bill,' he said.

'What, Bill has something for me?'

Lindsay handed me an envelope. I peeled back the seal, wondering if I was getting pranked, but it was an envelope full of cash.

'Oh my god.' I pulled the money from the envelope to count it.

'One thousand is what you need to reach your target right? Bill wanted to give it to you.'

'Wow, that is very generous of him.' I was overwhelmed.

Bill had become a much-loved figure around town throughout the shoot, even earning the nickname of Broken Hill Bill by locals. He was often sighted walking the streets on a Sunday and was a regular at the Silly Goat, a café in Argent Street that the film's cast and crew frequented.

Bill Nighy is still one of my favourites, not just for his incredible acting talent, but also for his kindness and respect to everyone he works with, no matter their position. The realisation came suddenly: WE DID IT! It seemed so impossible, but the community came together and made it happen, and I learned two more valuable lessons....

Sometimes you have to jump before you're ready, and showing up really is the key to success!

The final week of filming ended on a high note. I jumped in as an extra one night when some local talent didn't turn up. I managed to wiggle my curvy body into a pair of pants two sizes too small with Greg cheering me on.

'You've got this! Suck it in Sista.'

I arrived on set, to the surprise of the cast and crew, and was placed next to Billy, much to our amusement, in matching search and rescue outfits.

Victoria Hill and Kelton Pell, other leading cast members, were equally amused when they recognised me in their scene. Martin Sacks, Anthony Gooley, Ben Wood, and Julia Billington were also in the cast, all of whom I had gotten to know over the period of the shoot.

You become a family on these away jobs, and there was a tinge of sadness that the shoot was almost over. Soon everyone would go their separate ways. It had been the most incredible working experience of my life; I truly had been living the dream.

Gil, Jeannie and I had the honour of visiting Interhealth before our departure from town to see firsthand the delivery of eight djembe drums. The local newspaper captured the moment and ran the story on the front page with the headline 'Drumming Up Vital Support'.

Support is vital, and sometimes it takes a community to make things happen. JBJ was right, projects really are made possible by partnerships. We are stronger together!

Bizzy Bee and Becky Boo

Gil, Jeannie and I donating the drums for the Banging the Drum for Brain Injury program

Working with Bill Nighy

In my extras costume on Buckley's Chance with Sandy Stevens

CHAPTER TWENTY-ONE

Back to the Bush

When I returned to Brisbane, I was eager for my first cuddle with baby Aliana, who was now thriving. I can't describe the love I felt as a grandparent, and the wonder of seeing my own child become a parent. I was looking for work again. I reached out to all my Gold Coast contacts but couldn't get another film gig, so I packed my bag and returned to my seismic family. There were two crews running; the big team were already out on a job, so I was placed on the smaller crew and, lucky me, I was the only female amongst twenty blokes. This next run would be the most challenging yet.

I was back with Wayno, Kenny and Petey, but most of my other mates were on the other crew. We had a lot of new people, including a guy called Chris who liked rap. We became instant friends, with a shared love of poetry and the spoken word.

The following three months were spent working in extreme heat, with 40-plus degree temperatures on average in Central Queensland and the Northern Territory. Our lavish accommodation in Chinchilla was a distant memory. We stayed in camps, on stations, and in the isolated and remote Heartbreak Hotel at Cape Crawford, which also has a campground. I had been saying over and over in my mind 'Elvis, Elvis, Elvis' in an attempt to use the law of attraction to guide me to a job on Baz Lurhman's *Elvis* movie, about to begin filming on the Gold Coast. Instead, I found myself standing in front of a painting of Elvis Presley at the Heartbreak Hotel in the middle of nowhere!

You have to be specific Belinda, I berated myself.

This was an especially hard job, with the remote location, the extreme heat and bare necessities at camp. Our rooms had only a single bed and a bar fridge. No desk, television or ensuite: we instead used the outdoor amenities that were shared with other travellers. My donga was in the middle of my work mates', which I believe was for safety.

In an effort to lift team morale during what was going to be a very long month, I suggested we make a short horror movie in the evenings at camp. We were at the perfect location after all. I spread the word that I would be holding auditions one evening in an open space next to the car park at 7 pm and anyone interested in being part of the film should meet me there.

You could have knocked me down with a feather when I rounded the corner of the accommodation block to see twelve willing participants ready to launch their acting careers in what we called a Z grade horror film: *Camp Find Yourself.*

Jay, who was playing camp counsellor Mitch, could not get through his one and only line that night: *My element is water, I am going to connect you with your inner emotions,* without laughing, which had us all in hysterics. No careers would be launched on this project, but it provided some light relief after the long hard days.

Despite my attempts to make the most of those days, I felt my time in seismic was coming to an end. I was in perimenopause so my periods were all over the place and, often finding myself in the middle of nowhere, had to make do when my irregular periods arrived. Once I'd swapped bags when my period came early, and I had no supplies and no access to any in the middle of the bush. The only solution I could think of was to make a pad out of a plastic bag and a bandage from the first aid kit! It was a very uncomfortable day, and my patience was wearing thin.

Wayno had heard whispers and called me over one morning.

'I heard you are thinking of leaving us.'

'You heard right. All I want is fucking toilet – I'm too old for this shit!'

Like a protective big brother, Wayno offered a reassuring hug.

This would be the last seismic job. Even though I found aspects of the job personally challenging, the mateship and empowerment was a gift I'll treasure always. At a time when I was distrusting of men, I regained my trust by working with a team in some of the most remote locations and challenging conditions. Once, when a new crew member was being sleazy, I told him I was moving to another table because I was not going to listen to his inappropriate comments. Every other man at that table also got up and moved in solidarity and support. The company never hired him again.

Buzz, Bolly, Wayno, Kenny, Owie, Dr Strong, Petey and Chris were my brothers and helped me heal. I also worked with some amazing women: Kylie, Cassie, Barb, Sonya, Bec and I were all forging our own paths and, as much as I loved my band of brothers, it was always great when there was another female to chat with on the crew. We nicknamed the company Girlseis.

When I returned from the last hitch at Cape Crawford, I began chasing down leads for another film job. Jason called and said *RFDS* – Royal Flying Doctor Service – was coming back to Broken Hill to film a new series and asked if I wanted my name thrown into the ring.

'Yes please.'

The next thing I knew I was picking up a hire car and was on the road again to Broken Hill, this time to work on a television series. It was early 2020 so the pandemic was in its initial phase, and everything was uncertain. I only made it halfway before being turned back. The series was put on hold and borders began closing around Australia. I made it back across the Queensland border just before it closed.

My feelings of anger and injustice rose again. The government offered to double jobseeker payments and launched various other schemes. I needed assistance along with so many people in the country, but it was also a clear admission that the existing benefit was in no way enough for anyone to live on.

RFDS was one of the first series in the country to go back into production while a lot of the country was still in lockdown because there had been no cases of covid in Broken Hill. Our little cast and crew had to isolate for two weeks on arrival and live in a bubble for the entire shoot without returning home.

We became a film family that I stuck with for many years after the close bonds formed during those uncertain times. I'd heard a lot about Ross Allsop, one of the kindest and best line producers/producers in the business. Working for him is always a privilege. He makes every member of the crew feel valued, which is why people stick with him for so long. Like his production coordinator Erin, production secretary Emily, seasoned runner Denley and location manager Nicci. They welcomed me into the crew with open arms.

I became fast friends with the unit department; they take care of everyone on set and at Unit Base where all the film trailers are set up. They make sure the facilities are always clean and tidy and there is always tea and coffee on hand and also offer a friendly ear. They hold everything together on location. I would often raid their not-so-secret stash of lollies in the unit truck to get my red frog fix at the end of the day when I was waiting for the evening rushes.

I also became an honorary member of the costume department. Michael, Nee and Ali all hailed from Melbourne, and they were counting their blessings they weren't in Victoria during lockdown. They brought a lot of colour, not just to the costumes, but also to the town and to my life personally.

Madi, the costume standby, approached me one day with the idea to organise a girls' night and asked if I knew of any entertainers we could hire for the night.

'No strippers if that's what you mean, but I know a magnificent drag queen.'

Shelita Buffet put on one of the best night's entertainment, we all agreed, we had ever experienced. We bonded over silly games like putting the ring on the penis on people's heads. We all laughed until we cried. Everyone still talks about this night, a favourite memory, and Shelita Buffet was hands down a better host than any stripper.

Hudson had shown incredible strength and maturity during his teenage years and continued to forge ahead despite all the usual hurdles, but he had hit a wall and was questioning what he wanted to do with his life.

I still felt like I had failed him and recognised that he'd missed out on his parents being fully present at a time when it should have been his turn. I now knew how important it was to acknowledge this, so the feelings didn't manifest as worthlessness or crippling fear – feelings I understood only too well.

I called Ross and asked him if it would be possible for me to bring Hudson with me on our next TV gig in Alice Springs and if he could volunteer as an intern on the show. Ross had no hesitation in saying yes, so the only thing left to do was convince this city slicker kid to leave his comfort zone and relocate for months to the centre of Australia.

I began the conversation with Hudson by acknowledging that, over the preceding ten years, I was not as present as I should have been emotionally and, at times, physically. I knew he understood why, but that didn't change the absence he would have felt during my advocacy work and my relationship with Wayman.

I acknowledged that he must have felt overlooked and isolated at times and apologised for any pain I may have caused him, even though unintentional. During Dylan and Miki's teenage years our house was a hub of laughter and mateship for them and their friends. Hudson had gone through his parents' separation at ten, his brother's near death at twelve, and the years of rehab that followed, as well as the loss of our family home. Throughout he remained focused on his intent to study crime and justice, and never gave me one day of trouble. It was remarkable he had gotten this far before his wheels fell off.

I shared with Huddo the feelings of anxiety I had experienced at various points in my life and explained to him that I had only broken through by feeling the fear and doing it anyway. With repetition comes familiarity, and with familiarity comes confidence. Strength comes from overcoming what we didn't think we could.

I said I believed we needed some time together; that it was his turn for it to be all about him and told him of my plan for him to come to Alice and volunteer on the show.

Even though it was way out of his comfort zone, Huddo came, and it was a turning point for him. He interned on the show in the art department during pre-production before Ross put him on the payroll full-time as an art assistant. He went from sleeping all day to rising before the sun came up, working a long day on set, and ending his day at the gym, and he dragged me along also. We would arrive home exhausted, eat dinner, and go straight to bed ready to do it all over again the following day.

We were staying in a little cabin at the caravan park. This had its moments because we didn't each have our own space and I was studying for a postgraduate certificate in Creative Business at the time. Half my weekend was spent catching up on lectures. It required great discipline from us both. For me to focus when I was tired and for him to keep quiet in that small space while I had Zoom meetings and watched pre-recorded lectures.

Sundays were our favourite day. We'd go exploring all the wondrous national parks that surround Alice. It was a magical, healing time for us. We travelled from Tjoritja/West

McDonnell National Park and took a chopper tour over the top of Kings Canyon. The highlight was visiting Uluru on a rainy weekend. We got to see water cascading off the rock, one of the most glorious moments of my life, and I was so blessed to share it with my Huddo.

We shared another epic film experience in 2022 when I achieved my lifelong dream of working on a *Mad Max* movie. I had been offered a transport gig on *Furiosa: A Mad Max Saga*, for the Broken Hill portion of the shoot! I was supposed to be a driver but ended up working in the transport office instead. It was the biggest, craziest film shoot I have ever experienced. The circus literally moved into Broken Hill when the production set up a big circus tent, our base camp, out at Mundi Mundi.

It was a huge job logistically, but we had the most amazing drivers in our transport hub. We had to bring in motorhomes to house the 500-man crew because there wasn't enough accommodation in town. The usually quiet main street of the Hill resembled a bustling city on weekends.

My two supervisors, Paul 'Wamby' Wambach and Richie Rich Miller taught me a lot in the fast-paced madness that was the transport hub. Wamby was a firm believer in people doing things in a way that worked to their strengths, which enabled me to achieve to my best capacity. Sandy from *Buckley's* had recommended me for the job and insisted Wamby hire me, so it is thanks to her I got to fulfill this lifelong dream. The other lifelong dream I was able to fulfill was meeting George Miller. One night his driver had to wrap so as not break turn around (film crew need a minimum ten hours between shifts) so I was given the pickup instead. In one short car ride from the production office to his accommodation I was able to thank George for making my filmmaking dream come true. A moment I will always treasure.

The crazy vehicles on the film were unbelievable and so was getting the opportunity to see George Millar directing Anya Taylor Joy and Chris Hemsworth in my hometown. I remembered the little girl who'd dreamed of this moment but thought it was an unachievable dream.

The best part of the experience was being able to share it with Miki and Huddo who were both on crew. It was hard for Miki to be away from D and their pooch Dante, but she couldn't turn down the opportunity to work on such a massive production.

It was the first time we worked together on a film and was another full-circle moment for me remembering how I started down this path after working on Miki's school plays.

Hudson and I only worked on the Broken Hill portion of the shoot, but Miki went on to Sydney and did the entire film. During this time, she was going through IVF, having to inject herself with four needles a day whilst working long hours on set. She had been diagnosed with a low egg count and the ovaries of a forty year old. I had always taken for granted my ability to conceive; watching my daughter fight for her right to be a mother under some difficult circumstances was a testament to her strength and resilience.

The IVF was successful and nine months later, I was present to see my daughter bring her own into this world. Adelena (after Grandma Addie) Blossom was born on the 1st of July, 2023, making me Nanny B to three beautiful girls with Dylan and Chrissy having had Harper Lynn join their family in 2022. Being a nana is the best gig in the world.

Outback adventures with Hudson

CHAPTER TWENTY-TWO

Ballet for Brain Injury

On a high from the success of the Banging the Drum fundraising campaign, I launched straight into the next one. I had learned from my first experience that the research component was essential if we wanted the program to be received by the medical community, and therefore accessible to people Australia-wide. And, as I like to think without limits, worldwide! I'd researched the effects of dance on brain health, after reading about the benefits of dance for Parkinson's disease, with the idea of starting a dance rehabilitation class for people with brain injury. Given that both conditions affected the brain, I felt sure the outcomes being reported for people with Parkinson's disease would be similar to those living with a brain injury.

I approached Queensland Ballet's community engagement officer to discuss my idea. Martha was a gifted dancer with a focus on the benefits of dance in health, and keen to explore this idea further. So I enlisted a third party, Professor Elizabeth Kendall, chair of the Hopkins Centre and founder of many rehabilitation projects. She had an impressive body of work, with a focus on research and resilience. We formed a strong, collaborative team for the project, called 'Ballet for Brain injury' between my company, Citrine Sun Entertainment, Martha at Queensland Ballet, and Professor Elizabeth Kendall representing Griffith University and the Hopkins Centre. This would my first experience as Project Development

Manager and I was thrilled to be collaborating with such strong corporate partnerships.

The program needed to be evidence-informed, so Elizabeth enlisted Professor Naomi Sunderland as Lead Investigative Researcher to head up our scoping literature review on enablers and barriers for people with brain injury and their carers. The review was led by honours student Joel Spence and me as a co-investigator. The review was funded by Queensland Conservatorium Research Centre. The evidence from this review informed the ten-week Ballet for Brain Injury Pilot Program that also had input from Queensland Ballet teaching artists and clinicians Kerry Read and Peter Irving, physiotherapist and occupational therapist, respectively.

We tailored the dance program to engage people living with a brain injury, and their carers/family/support worker. Arts-based movement approaches are increasingly recognised as accessible, holistic, and potentially empowering resources for brain injury patients and others who experience disability.

Dance has been proven to help people surviving brain injury to re-inhabit their bodies. It also helps in coping with emotional, cognitive and physical impairments from a brain injury. The artistic and creative nature of ballet and other dance forms allows brain injured participants to use their own life experience to inspire movement and dance.

The ten-week pilot program was conducted at Queensland Ballet's West End studios from April to June 2021 using ballet-based movement and music enabling participants to experience the enjoyment, creative expression and well-being benefits of dance. All project partners, participants and staff involved in the Ballet for Brain Injury program were pioneers, and the program brought new insight into the benefit of ballet for brain injury survivors and their communities.

I'm a firm believer in the power of film and television to elevate a story. I also have a strong drive to become an impact producer, so I raised funds to record the program's progress on film which was primarily sponsored by Kerry Read. Jacques was my cinematographer and Miki was assistant director.

I interviewed some of the participants who bravely shared their experience of trialling the ten-week pilot program. They also shared some of the difficulties and barriers they had faced in their own journeys with brain injury, and as carers.

I had put in a request with Queensland Ballet to interview their Artistic Director Li Cunxin in the doco. Li made a special appearance to speak of QB's commitment to accessibility of their arts/health programs and the importance of disability inclusion.

It was extraordinary meeting a man whose resilience had inspired me. I had read Li's book *Mao's Last Dancer* and had seen the film many times. If anyone had told me I would one day be directing Li in a short film I would never have believed them.

He was extremely gracious, and generous with his time. We exchanged a few words privately before he was whisked away. I added another momentous moment to my bank of moments: *collect moments, not things.*

Other precious moments were the interviews with the participants themselves, who reported many benefits, including:

The program created a sense of community and identity for brain injury survivors.

Improvements with balance, coordination and memory.

Growing self-confidence and self-esteem over the course of the program.

Pride - Participants were dancers at a prestigious cultural organisation, not patients attending a rehabilitation session.

Their stories were woven through our short film *QB Ballet for Brain Injury* which made the finals of the World Health Organisation's *Health for All International Short Film Festival* in 2022. The clip was listed on WHO's website promoting the program and the research, creating awareness on an international level. The power of film at its best!

Classes continue to run weekly at Queensland Ballet, and the program has now expanded into hospitals. The power of we again. I will always be grateful to Professor Elizabeth

Kendall and Martha Godber for listening to my idea. We collectively took action and breathed it to life.

One night as I was driving through Fortitude Valley in Brisbane, I saw a giant billboard by Griffith University which read WHAT IF BALLET COULD HELP WITH BRAIN INJURY? I sat underneath the sign thinking how it all started with me asking that very question. I realised that we are far more powerful than we believe, and just have to be brave, to feel the fear and do it anyway. In January 2024, I was honoured with the Medal of the Order of Australia for service to community health. Nobody becomes an advocate or activist because they want to receive awards, but it's great to have a spotlight shone on the work and the cause. It made me reflect on what can be achieved when you truly believe. For me, there's no greater proof than walking beside Dylan on his journey. Watching my son lose his identity made me realise that one of the greatest freedoms is to be who we truly are; the only way to change our path is to change the way we think and feel. I am not diminishing what this took, but when I look back I realise how powerful Dylan's thoughts were in his healing. In creating a world of fantasy and adventure during those early days post-coma, he was changing his emotional state. By taking on the persona of Iron Man and Robert Downey, he elevated himself to superhero at a time when he was most vulnerable.

Dylan has overcome insurmountable obstacles during his recovery, though there are invisible barriers he lives with every day.

We need to change the narrative around brain injury. It can be a permanent disability, the daily impact of which is dependent on stressors in the individual's life and environment. The notion that only people severely impacted require formal support is false. Equity is needed in access to support for people who are largely independent but require some assistance in the home and in the workplace. Communities need to work together to alleviate the stressors so that brain injury survivors can live with dignity and thrive. This will lessen some of the burden placed on unpaid carers. **Our emotional state affects brain structure and well-being. Feelings are consistent with thoughts, so we can change our physical health depending on what we think, and therefore feel. Our brains don't know the difference between what is happening now, and what is perceived to be happening.**

Fear, anxiety and stress create dis-ease in the body and shut down areas of the brain. This is what happened to me when I reached overload, after running on adrenaline for years.

There have been moments over the past twelve years when my emotions have felt like an out-of-control freight train, which derailed more than a few relationships. Some people come into our lives for a season, others for a reason. I'm grateful to all those who crossed my path because each has given me something. I hope I have given in return.

I am learning, daily, to observe my mind. This is equally as important as working on the body. The greatest gift in my life is my kids and grandkids. They are my crew! Huddo has continued to work in film and television whilst studying towards his dream career in policing.

Miki has been working on her acting career, studying the craft. After a second IVF journey, she will soon be a mum to two precious daughters.

Dylan is still working at the PA Hospital and is a loving father to his two beautiful girls, Aliana and Harper. He and Chrissy do an amazing job of co-parenting their gorgeous girls. He works hard every day for the life he has built post-injury.

And me, I'm still trying to figure out what I want to be when I grow up. I am fifty and I still don't know. One thing I do know is that you are never too old to change your path. I have felt the all-encompassing fear of not knowing if my child would survive. I, like many, understand the fear of not knowing where my next paycheck was coming from, and when. I have known living in a home where I wasn't free to be myself and didn't feel safe.

I have made many mistakes but I am not my past. Change can be uncomfortable, especially when we hold a mirror up to ourselves and realise we have patterns of behaviour that inform our choices. Changing lifelong patterns is not easy.

The arts and health are inexplicably linked. Stories have the power to shape who we are and, research has shown, impact on society. When we connect emotionally with a character on screen it can shift viewpoints so 'who' is telling the stories we watch is important!

I finally stopped 'Chasing Jon' and started writing my own story, this book. I've also been developing a television series based on my experience as an older woman thrown into a hyper-masculine mining world. I wanted to showcase the beauty of the vast Australian outback, and the challenges faced by the authentic Aussies who live and work in some of the harshest and most remote locations in the country.

Out there, crews become more than colleagues, they become family. Looking out for your mate can mean the difference between life and death. At a time when we're so focused on gender roles and identities, being amongst a team of men in the middle of nowhere I realised that I could be strong without being hard and learned to embrace my emotional side as a strength not a weakness.

I began developing my television series concept when I was working on *RFDS* in Broken Hill. I printed off photos and made character and plot cards that I pinned to cork boards. It was my first job working for Ross and, once I got to know him better, I mentioned I had an idea for a TV series, and I would love to get his feedback. 'Of course, B,' he said. 'I'll be in the office Saturday morning.' So I packed up all my cork boards that Saturday, excited and nervous that I was about to share my idea with one of Australia's most successful producers.

I entered the office, juggling and dropping the cork boards and announcing my entry. Ross tried to stifle a laugh and I cringed internally.

'You okay B, you need some help?'

'No no. I'm all good thanks.'

I took a seat in front of his desk and, nervously, began showing him the boards, one by one. I explained the premise and talked about the characters based on my real-life work buddies.

'This is good B, it's got legs! Have you thought of showing it to Imo?'

Imogen Banks was the executive producer and creator of *RFDS* as well as *Offspring* among others. I was a big fan of her work and had heard her speak at a producer's workshop in 2017 when I was on my 'Chasing Jon' journey. Every time I saw her in the *RFDS* production office I'd get tongue-tied and didn't know what to say, despite her being the most approachable executive producer I have, to this day, ever met.

'Imogen Banks! I can't just approach Imogen Banks and ask her to take a look at my idea.'

On cue, Imogen walked through the front door of the production office and approached Ross's desk to talk with him. She glanced down at my boards and asked what they were all about.

'Just an idea I've been developing for a show,' I replied sheepishly.

'Looks interesting,' she said, her gaze sweeping across the boards.

As she left, she paused and turned.

'I'd be happy to take a look at that, if you want me to. Just shoot me an email and we can arrange a catch up.'

I turned to Ross, who looked very pleased. 'Well, there you go,' he said.

'Oh my god.'

I left that office floating. Imogen became a great mentor. She put me forward for an incredible opportunity to develop my series in a new Graduate Certificate in Creative Business that included Tenacity Labs mentoring program. This was facilitated by Dr David Court who had taught the Masters of Filmmaking at AFTRS, the Australian Film Television and Radio School. David taught several of Australia's most successful producers, including Imogen. He also worked in financing films.

David shared his wealth of knowledge with us all.

It was a challenging year of formal study whilst working full-time. But it changed the way I viewed myself. I realised I was capable of more than I thought, and that I could learn things I'd previously not believed I could.

It was in Alice Springs, working on the ABC job with Ross, that the idea of writing a book was suggested by Imogen. She came to visit us one weekend in the NT and suggested there was a lot more to my story than just the FIFO chapter, and that a book would allow me to share it all. 'Gosh, I don't think I would have time to write a book with everything else going on.'

My image of writers was the solitary figure at a desk in some cabin in the woods with peace and quiet. There was no way I could ever find the time to write a book.

But once the seed was planted, I couldn't shake the idea from my mind. I did want to write my story, even if just for my children and grandchildren. And, throughout my life, nothing made true sense to me until I wrote it down.

With the Ballet for Brain Injury Pilot Program complete and my ABC job behind me, I was looking for the next film and TV job opportunity. But really all I wanted was to begin writing my book.

I always meditate in the shower, visualising the water clearing away the stress from my body and carrying it down the plughole, but I began adding a new intention: 'I am a money magnet, money flows into my bank account.'

I would repeat this, visualising the digits of my account balance going up. I told Miki of my new little exercise, and she told me she thought I was nuts.

'Whatever works for you Bizjovi!'

Weeks later I was spending the evening at Kyla's beach shack located at Nobby's Beach on the Gold Coast. We were long overdue for a girls' catch up after my extended period in Alice. My phone pinged and I opened the email. It was Imogen suggesting I check my bank account. She had generously gifted me funds to buy me time to start writing my book. It was a gift, she said.

The greatest gift was what she said: that my story was important and needed to be told, and that it was enough. To have someone of Imo's experience believe in me enabled me to believe in myself. It also gave a huge boost to my faith in humanity. Everybody's story is important, and so are the stories we tell ourselves every day. Our inner dialogue instructs the body to produce hormones and emotions that can harm or heal.

It's taken me a long time to understand the importance of being a friend to myself and to learn the art of self-forgiveness; to love my ageing body, the vehicle that allows me to move through my time here on earth.

I finally understand. Peace and love aren't something you find, but what you are; what you bring to the world through your presence.

Ballet for Brain Injury – Photo credit Queensland Ballet

Me, Miki and Jacques with Li Cunxin AO

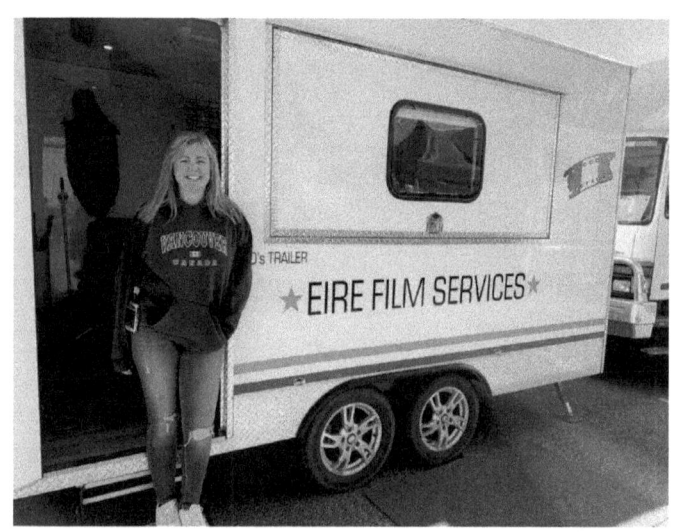

Working in film and television – a childhood dream come true

Acknowledgements

I'd like to express my deepest appreciation to the following people, without whom this book would not have been possible.

To my son Dylan, thank you for your blessing to share some of the most intimate moments of your life, from the tragic to the triumphant. Your strength and resilience are truly remarkable as is the love you have for your girls. It lights up your very soul.

To my feisty, talented, empathetic and compassionate Miki, thanks for being a beacon of light and strength when I struggled to find my own. You took on the role of a fierce Mumma bear long before you became one to your two beautiful girls.

To my wingman Hudson, you chose to turn some challenging times into motivation to make a difference in this world for the better. Grateful for the special adventures we have shared the past few years working together in film and proud of the man you have become.

To my mum, Frannie, for being a consistent source of kindness, grace, compassion and companionship.

My dad, Garry, for showing me the importance of lying under a star-filled sky.

To my precious grandbabies, may you always know the importance of YOUR story.

Imogen Banks, without you there would be no book. Thank you for seeing and believing in my story and me.

Kylie Fitzpatrick, my editor/writing coach extraordinaire. For teaching me the art of writing. Your skill, experience and patience guided me on one of the hardest yet most rewarding journeys of my life.

Suellen Dainty, thank you for the countless hours of support and mentorship you kindly donated to a total stranger because you saw potential in my writing.

Frank Hough and Sharon Carleton, for connecting the dots, it's because of you the final pieces of the puzzle fell into place.

To my family and the friends who became family, you have all been an integral part of my story, and my life. I would love to have written about the treasured life experiences I have had with every single one of you but the memories we share are written on my heart always.

To the doctors, nurses and clinicians at the Princess Alexandra Hospital for the lifesaving care you gave my son and continue to give.

To Bob Mander, Warren Lindsay and Russell Roberts for being a lifeline for Dylan when he needed it. You will never know how much your kindness and care impacted him during the most difficult of days and helped him rebuild his life again.

Kerry Read, how do I even begin to thank you. You have been by my side throughout Dylan's entire recovery offering support and advice to both him and me. Without you, we wouldn't be where we are today.

Thank you to the Queensland Government and Logan City Council for supporting the development process of this book through their Regional Arts Development Fund (RADF).

Finally, thank you to Bon Jovi for the music that touched my heart when nothing else could.

Endorsements

Belinda Adams is a force of nature with a heart and a mind to make a difference. This book tells the fantastic story of her fight for her injured son and the extraordinary journey that resulted.

Dr David Court – Executive Director, Compton School

Belinda's book is the story of a mother's love and devotion to her son after he sustained a brain injury, and the power music had on their journey to healing. It will be an inspiration to all who read it.

Dyna Carr – Live Nation Brisbane Rep

Belinda tells her inspiring story of never giving up hope, of triumph against all odds and using that experience to help others. She is passionate about improving the lives of those with an invisible disability and highlighting the barriers for those who care for them.

Kerry Read – Principal Physiotherapist at Headline Physiotherapy

Mick and I with our dad Gary

My brother Mick and I in the 80's

Skydiving

Bizz, Mick & Bek growing up in Broken Hill

Growing up in Broken Hill

Me, Mum & Miki – 3 generations working at Merthyr Law

Hudson, Miki, myself and Dylan

With some of my film family in the Northern Territory

Kyla and I on an adventure in the bus

Speaking at WIFT panel discussion Inclusion by design at the Gold Coast Film Festival in 2019 alongside Katrina Irawati Graham, Angel Dixon OAM and Steph Dower

Me and Mick with our much-loved Grandma Addie

Ready to rock at a Bon Jovi concert

Me and my Dad

Desi J Johnson – Forever in our hearts

www.ingramcontent.com/pod-product-compliance
Lightning Source LLC
Chambersburg PA
CBHW061744070526
44585CB00025B/2795